What Others Are Saying About SHIFT...

In this book, my friend Phil cleverly combines the power of narrative and the power of timely ideas to make a point about ministry impact. He is not only a warm-hearted leader ministering in a local church, but also proves to be a good guide for others taking their churches on a similar journey.
 -**Alan Hirsch,** Award winning author on missional movements, Founder, Forge Mission Training Network and 100 Movements.
alanhirsch.org

Upon previewing Shift, my immediate impression was that somehow Phil Underwood had been able to interview 80 percent of the pastors and church staff members in America and had discerned from them the kind of dissatisfaction that arises when someone realizes there must be a better way, but is not sure exactly what it is. His perceptive analysis and subsequent insightful recommendation for church redirection is a spiritual prescription that makes abundant sense.
 -**Dr. Mark L. Williams,** General Overseer, Church of God, Cleveland, TN

"I love what Phil is doing with this new book of his. I know the wonderful fulfillment and yet the dizzying disappointment of building a large church, with an attractional model. Multitudes of church leaders, over the years, came to see how we were doing, what we were doing. However, the more we succeeded, the more I grew suspicious, that we were grasping a part of what the church was all about, and yet were missing an important piece of it. In recent years there have been several great books around how to develop a healthy rhythm around the "gathered" and "scattered" church models.... and what does it mean to live missionally. But this is the first time I've seen a book try to personalize it all in a story, that is actually the personal story of so many of us leaders. In someone's personal story (even when it's fictionalized) we can find much more of ourselves, than in primary instruction or teaching. This book accomplishes that. I've known Phil for a couple of decades and know firsthand the grand passion he carries, to help facilitate the experience of an impactful church. Read this book and see if you can't discover even more of what God might be saying to you."

-David Loveless, Co-founder Live True
youlivetrue.com

Phil Underwood is that *rara avis*—that rare bird among consultants. He not only understands the nature of the church as a missional community; he can read and braille a church culture in record time, and help you discover yourself how to turn monuments and museums into movements, and mission fields into mission forces. His spirit is affirming, encouraging, upbeat, and you always want to be around him because of his inspirations for your aspirations. If you want someone to lead you or your faith community away from the harbor of maintenance and safety and towards open waters of mission, especially the "oceanic" feelings that come from living as Jesus lived, then Phil's your guide.

-Dr. Leonard Sweet Author, Futurist
leonardsweet.com

Phil has a passion for developing leaders that are making a difference for the kingdom.

-Bill Couchenour, Director of Development, Exponential

Phil Underwood is a man with outstanding vision, focus, and drive to get his clients to a new level. Those who work with him, and those who know him, see in him a true leader in every sense of the word - someone who won't place on you the lastest, greatest, trendy solutions and answers; rather someone who will guide you and lead you to discover yours.

-Bruce Barnard, Mission New York, New York City

ISBN-10: 0692500421
ISBN-13: 978-0692500422 (CRM reFocusing)

Church Resource Ministries

ChurchNEXT

1240 N Lakeview Ave # 120, Anaheim, CA 92807

www.crmleaders.org

reFocusing

a Ministry of CRM / ChurchNEXT Collective

www.refocusing.org

714.779.0370

Sam Metcalf, President

Helping leaders and churches worldwide succeed at
making disciples and transforming their communities.

SHIFT

Gearing Your Heart to Lead God's Mission

Phil Underwood

With Contribution from the CRM reFocusing Team:
David Zimmerman, Kirk Kirlin, Gary Janetzke
Matt Weston, Mark Goeser

With Special Thanks to
Leslie Spurrier
for Creative & Editing Assistance

reFocusing is a Missional Advancement Team
Operating as Part of Church Resource Ministries'
ChurchNEXT Collective

SHIFT

Chapters

Foreword

Bubbling in the deep cauldron of personal longing, every pastor I know yearns to see the lives of people and the community where they live transformed by the life-giving presence of Jesus. Their calling into ministry came with a blend of angst and hope. *Angst* about the stunted experience of following Jesus common to so many churchgoers and about the under-experienced power of the gospel in a broken world. But, *hope* anchored in the God of resurrection who invites us to walk in his easy yoke every day.

However, launched with dreams of changing the world, many pastors these days feel like they are stuck spinning plates. One pastor confessed not long ago that he never imagined being a pastor would mean he spent his days "clicking keys on a keyboard."

Pastors are not alone. The long dull ache so many pastors live with is mirrored by the fatigue and disillusionment of ministry and business leaders of every type. While the church of the west has been the engine of the global mission movement for 150 years, we have lost the home court advantage right where we live. Where once the church was a place that people of all kinds turned to for spiritual answers in times of need, today our culture has turned away, and even grown suspicious of the church.

So what is a local church to do? Where do we start? Or, maybe even more importantly, who will walk with us as we seek to navigate the changing currents of the waters we find ourselves in?

Leaders don't have to go it alone. In fact, more than twenty years ago, those of us at CRM discovered that the transformation of a local church and its impact starts in the life of leaders. Ministry methods, preaching skills, and church programs are all worthy of attention, but the real catalyst for unleashing a fresh work of Christ is the fresh work of Jesus in the life of a leader.

For twenty years our reFocusing ministry staff have empowered leaders to encounter Jesus and his perspective on their leadership in a fresh way. We create relationships and learning experiences that are safe places for leaders in the trenches of ministry. In the process, calling is clarified, character is deepened, skills are developed, church members are mobilized to live on mission, and courage is born to lead congregations through change and out into their communities.

There are new questions that need to be asked. It is rather easy to ask questions about the health, effectiveness, or adjustments needed in our existing programs. But, navigating our way through an era of quantum level change calls for revisiting the questions of a missiologist.

Asking difficult questions in the context of a safe supportive relationship opens up room for creative thinking. But, don't misunderstand, the questions that leaders need to wrestle with these days are not only tough, their answers can feel threatening to established ways of doing things. A few of the significant questions we need to revisit include questions like these.

- What does ministry success really look like? Not, what does ministry activity look like, but what are the outcomes of ministry we are striving for? To say it a different way, what are the metrics we should be measuring?

- What would it look like if maturity as a follower of Christ was defined more by the way we participate in the missional agenda of Christ than by the quantity of biblical data we have mastered?

- How might we begin to engage a lost and broken world that has turned a deaf ear to the rhetoric of the church, though they really only know a caricature of Jesus?

- What will it take to normalize equipping and mobilizing people for ministry "out there" beyond the walls of the church?

- How can leaders attend to the care of their souls and the primacy of their relationship with Christ while giving leadership to the constant and demanding challenges of ministry?

None of the questions are simple, just as the complexities of ministry leadership these days are not simple. There are no magic solutions and no quick fixes, but that doesn't mean there isn't hope. We have seen over and over again that the power of a safe relationship unleashes the creativity and possibilities that flow out of questions like these.

The story in this book invites you to see the journey of renewal through the eyes and heart of a local pastor. It will bring you into some of the common, but private, musings of a ministry leader. And I think you will taste the power of hope reborn.

This story of Michael Vinings represents the kind of work that our ChurchNEXT teams do every day here at CRM. We are a band of pioneering missionary teams that help leaders and churches worldwide, succeed at making disciples and transforming their communities. Our staff are some of the most godly and gifted ministry leaders I know and they chose to live this missionary calling because they love the church and those who lead her.

We believe God is building a revolutionary movement of hope through the church as it is and the church that could be. This book is an invitation to join that movement in a deeper way.

On behalf of the reFocusing Team and all the staff of ChurchNEXT, I invite you to dream anew about all that the church could be in the world we call home these days. If there are ways any of us can serve you in your journey, we would be delighted.

Dr. Gary Mayes
Executive Director, ChurchNEXT

Author: *DNA of a Revolution: 1st Century Breakthroughs that will transform the church;* and *DNA of a Revolution: The Small Group Experience.*

For more information about the mission and teams of ChurchNEXT: www.crmleaders.org/churchnext

Let every man abide in the calling wherein he is called
and his work will be as sacred as the work of the ministry.
It is not what a man does that determines whether
his work is sacred or secular, it is why he does it.
— A.W. Tozer, *The Pursuit of God*

Chapter 1

How Do You Spell Ministry? W-O-R-K?

The dull shapes of lifeless living room furniture melted into late-night shadows, while the icy glow of a full moon sliced through the darkness to illuminate the edge of the lone armchair in the corner. Coming home late for the third night in a row, Carol welcomed the dimness of the moon's glow, which subtly revealed a small plastic tea set abandoned on the floor in front of her feet. One false step would send Carol wincing in pain and most certainly mean a trip to the trash can for the flimsy tea set. Recently, four-year-old Naomi had taken to throwing impromptu tea parties before bedtime. Remembering this brought a tired smile to Carol's face as she

1

peeked through Naomi's door at the sleeping preschooler whose forehead was just visible above a thick, pink comforter.

Moving like the wisp of a shadow down the hall, Carol peered through another door into her son James' room. Just two-years-old, James was all dump trucks and dirt, diggers and dust. And noise. It seemed even in his sleep the little guy gently revved some unseen engine from under a blanket embroidered with tractors and all manner of farm equipment. "Love them," thought Carol, tenderly smiling, knowing that both her babies slept soundly.

Now, as Carol padded down the remainder of the dark hallway to the room she shared with her husband, she felt a familiar tensing of her body. A quickened heartbeat, an ever-growing knot in her stomach, small beads of perspiration beginning to blossom at the nape of her neck - all familiar symptoms of the same illness: ministry.

To be fair, it wasn't ministry itself that brought on these feeling of anxiety and dread. During her mid-twenties, right before she met her husband, Jerry, Carol traveled to Uganda and taught in a mission school for orphans affected by AIDS for six months. The miraculous progress of her students and the mutual affection they shared for one another sparked a fire she never knew existed. That experience moved her from being a marginal believer to feeling completely sold-out to God and his work. Tenderly caring for the orphans at school opened something up in Carol she had not known lay dormant for so long. From here her passion for children blossomed into a calling from God. She left a comfortable teaching job to look into options to serve God in ministry. One opportunity led to another, and now with two kids, a husband, and eight years under her belt she felt . . . none of the same fire for ministry as she once did.

Carol noticed the sag in her shoulders as her mind replayed this series of events. These days, God's work seemed concealed in the pile of paperwork on the corner of her desk, the mass of e-mails she answered daily, and the monotony of assembling weekly schedules, not to mention the steady drudgery of drumming up (begging, actually) volunteers. These days Carol felt more like a limp balloon devoid of all its air than a conquering hero for the faith.

Opening the door to her bedroom, Carol heard the soft sounds of her husband's rhythmical breathing. "Good, he's still sleeping," she thought. Her shoulders relaxed. She slipped off her shoes, eased out of her work clothes, and slipped into her pajamas. With the skill of a practiced CIA operative, she slowly lifted the covers on the bed and slipped between the sheets. Head on the pillow, deep sigh...

"Hey," came the voice – flat and irritated – from somewhere in the darkness.

"You're still up?" Carol asked. Shoulders tensed.

"Yeah, I guess I am, though it is 11:18 p.m., and I have to get up at 5:00 a.m. tomorrow to get to the site. I just figured if I wanted to see my wife at all, it'd have to be now." Jerry ended his comment with his usual "harrumph" which he reserved only for those moments in which he felt extremely annoyed.

"Well thanks so much for waiting up." Ever the people-pleaser, Carol didn't want to start an argument. "We ran really late at Christian Ed. tonight. Blaine had a new idea for VBS, but of course, Kim couldn't get on board with it. So I was running interference. You know how that goes. Anyway, it doesn't happen that often." Carol rolled over at this last statement, signaling that her part of the conversation came to an end.

Silence.

A dull muffling sound arose from Jerry's side of the bed as he slowly rolled out and gathered some covers.

"What are you doing?" Carol asked.

"I'm sleeping on the couch. I've really had enough."

"What are you talking about?" Carol, now wide-awake, felt panicked. This kind of drama was *not* Jerry. He seemed angry, really angry. But even worse, Carol detected a hint in his voice that betrayed…what? Defeat? Hopelessness? Ever since they met, Jerry served as Carol's rock. Always solid, always encouraging, always reliable. Carol often marveled at how God placed such a stalwart of a guy in her life. He never gave up on anything. Jerry was a fighter – to the end. He was the absolute perfect person for her. And now he was essentially holding up the white flag of surrender.

"Wait," she said, her voice held a pleading tone to it. "Can we talk or are you just going to give up and leave?"

"Give up!" Jerry answered, incredulously. "Carol, for the past two years you have been married to that church, your ministry. You have canceled plans, ditched get-togethers, and missed birthday parties – with your own kids – for the sake of your stupid ministry. You have been absent from more "family" meals than I can count, and I honestly can't remember the last time you and I had any time together – quality or otherwise!"

Though she did not think it possible, Jerry was actually seething. His teeth were bared, bits of white standing out from the blackness of the room. She could almost smell his ire, his resentment. While he continued his voice remained restrained, his tone did not.

"Every Sunday, you leave at the crack of dawn. We don't even see you at church, you're flittering everywhere – anywhere someone may need you. Heaven forbid somebody there solves a problem on his or her own! And you want to know what the worst part is?" Carol just stared blankly, unable to respond. "The worst part is that I don't even see you making a difference. I mean, how many kids come to know Jesus through that gigantic Easter egg hunt? Huh? All I see is a bunch of greedy neighborhood brats running away with bulging bags full of chocolate. And you," he paused to take a breath; Carol braced herself while he rolled on, "You're not the woman I married; the woman who was so in love with Jesus that she couldn't help but ooze affection and care for others." His voice fell to a hoarse whisper. "It just…it just breaks my heart to see how things have…" He broke off as the sound of Carol's own sobs echoed throughout the room, despite her attempt to stifle them with her pillow.

Jerry's voice seemed almost a vapor now, "Carol…I love the Lord with all my heart, you know I do, and I love you deeply, but this…this all has to stop. Things have to change."

***

As the sun sank below the horizon, the team began to move into high gear. The day's blistering heat meant that the crew needed to take longer, more frequent breaks, and now – almost two hours behind schedule – they pushed themselves to finish preparations in time for the show.

"Check, check, one…two…three…check, check, check." From a modest stage at the front of a huge white tent, a tall bean-pole of a man spoke into the microphone. In faded jeans, a white t-shirt, and canvas sneakers, one would never know this man was running the show. Until he opened his mouth, that is. Tapping the mic intermittently, his voice echoed throughout the confines of the arena. With seating for over 400, getting the perfect sound for this "intimate" concert was critical.

"Geez Alec, what are you doing back there!" barks the man. "We've got three hours until the concert, and we're already two hours behind. I'm still hearing a lot of feedback. Either take care of it, or find someone else who can. We cannot waste time because of your ego. This is not the moment for a lesson in patience or perseverance."

When Jonathan – the guy on stage – wanted perfection, he got it. A musical prodigy from an early age, reaching his high standards seemed like climbing to the summit of Mount Everest. But if anyone had a right to demand perfection, it was Jonathan. Upon graduation from high school, the natural musician spent five years in Nashville where he successfully recorded two albums. He played the guitar, piano, drums, and violin flawlessly on those albums and had since been a part of two major tours in the U.S. Retiring from the Nashville music scene, Jonathan continued to function at the top of his game as one of the most respected musicians in the area.

His years of concert experience gave him an edge in getting things together for today's performance. And while putting on this concert would be no small task, he felt up to the challenge. But then again, Jonathan always felt up to a challenge. That was part of Jonathan as well – the guy at the center of the action. Whatever Jonathan got his hands on, he commanded. Confident and capable, Jonathan naturally moved into the role of director or coordinator.

Typically, his ideas and plans get pushed through and successfully pulled off. Through the force of his will and the history of accomplishments, he motivated people to work hard in order to get some amazing results.

However, he also often left a wake of destruction in his path.

"Where is Marcus? Has anyone seen Marcus?" Jonathan never felt frantic at times like this. Inside his mind resided a kind of controlled peace. In the midst of chaos, he could return to that place of peace by exerting an iron arm of control over his circumstances. More control in times like this, more control.

Striding with his trademark long-legged gait, Jonathan snapped orders like a drill sergeant.

"Kaillee, I told you to e-mail Simeon about the band's change in arrival time and the need to run through a couple songs before the concert. He just texted me about it. What the heck? Get it done, now!"

"Trent, for the second time, you cannot have that light there. It throws an awful shadow and blocks the line of sight for a quarter of the audience. I swear we already had this conversation 30 minutes ago, and I told you what needed to happen."

"Look Sophie, I really don't want to hear about parking issues right now. Sort it out. That is why I hired you. If you can't take the responsibility then just leave. Man, I thought you people were supposed to be competent?"

"Marcus! Marcus! Where in the world is Marcus!"

Pulling off this event would be nothing short of a miracle, but Jonathan considered himself in the business of making miracles happen. Working with a steady stream of volunteers, he counted it no small task to pull off large-scale events using a team of inexperienced people. In times like these, he appreciated his ability to manage and get the job done.

The next two hours became a blur of trouble-shooting, fine tuning, executive directing, and micro-managing. Jonathan moved like magic; he was everywhere at once. During the final stages of preparation, Jonathan allowed himself a moment of quiet observation. Nothing, nothing brought him joy like the satisfaction of seeing an event come together. In the end, his team executed his directives flawlessly.

This was his bliss.

Now, as the band wrapped up their last practice set (of course, Jonathan directed that as well) and the instruments were hauled off stage until show time the lights dimmed. Jonathan saw a queue of people stretching through the parking lot and halfway down the block. Ambling backstage, he peeked from behind the curtain for a glimpse of concert-goers pecking through rows of chairs to find their seats. Loads of people had come out; the band would be playing to a packed house tonight. Of course Jonathan had expected nothing less.

Before the lights went down and the concert began, Jonathan gathered his team together for one final word. "Guys, it wasn't pretty today, but now it's done. Let this be a lesson to us. I'll be speaking with a few of you tomorrow – we'll need to make some changes around here if we want to continue with any level of success. But you all managed to get it together enough tonight to pull it off. Remember, when our church puts on things like this, it has to be perfect. This is the biggest outreach we've attempted so far and there is no room for error. Keep that in mind when we meet tomorrow to debrief about everything. Now, before the concert begins, let's take some time to thank God for everything. Let's pray."

***

The results were in. Evan and his family sat around a modest dinner table on Sunday afternoon. With a steaming pot roast on display in the center of the table, and Evan's three brothers salivating to take the first bite, each member of the family unfolded the pieces of paper held in their hands.

"So what did you get?" Evan asked aloud. Three weeks ago, the members of Evan's church took part in filling out a survey on spiritual gifts. Pastor Gary Borden was hoping to drum up a little more support for ministry: volunteers in the nursery had dipped to an all-time low, the trustees needed a couple more guys to help with the mowing, and the kitchen committee ended up short-handed for the annual spaghetti dinner fundraiser. Pastor Gary felt that if people saw they were "gifted" for these areas of service, they would jump right in to volunteer. Now, the Masterson family looked over the assessment detailing how God's Spirit equipped them.

"I got 'exhorting,'" volunteered Evan's mother, Sandra. "I guess it's good that I'm on the card committee then," she responded with feigned enthusiasm.

"I got 'intercession,'" noted Evan's older brother, Abe. "It's just too bad that I have wrestling practice on Wednesday nights and can't get to the prayer meeting. Anyway, I heard that the only people that go are the old ladies from church, and they just gossip about other people and try to disguise it as a prayer request."

"Abe!" scolded Sandra. "That's not fair of you to say! Where did you hear such nonsense anyway?"

"From Dad," Abe responded.

At that very moment, Evan's father, Paul Masterson, seemed to find something deeply fascinating in the contents of the paper in his hand and subsequently buried his nose in it. Raising his glance toward his wife and meeting her reproachful gaze, he shrugged his shoulders as if you say, "You know it's true."

"What was your gift Dad?" inquired Evan. Evan and his father had always been close. He admired his dad greatly. Paul Masterson had always been a wonderful supporter of all his sons, but in Evan he saw a real and sincere hunger for the Lord; he sought to encourage Evan to grow that hunger in any way he could.

"Oh, the usual I guess. I got 'service' again. I'm already part of one of the mowing crews," his voice drifted off. "Maybe I'll sign up to be an usher. I think they need some help now that Gilbert Forry passed on."

The wistfulness in his father's voice sent an aching twinge through Evan's heart. Evan could never remember a time when he didn't feel the close presence of Jesus and his Spirit. Baptized at age four, Evan knew without a doubt that God had a strong calling on his life. That's why it broke his heart to see other people struggling to find their place, to know their calling. Watching his father's bushy brows furrow in reflection, Evan sensed a distance between Christ's impact on his father's life and the way in which that impact expressed itself. In other words, Evan knew his dad passionately loved Jesus, he just couldn't find the right way to live it out.

"Dad," Evan began, reaching across the table to gently lay a hand on his father's arm, "Maybe that gifts test isn't the only way to figure out what God wants you to do. I mean, do you really want to be an usher and hand out bulletins? What do you feel God wants you to do?"

Paul patted Evan's hand appreciatively. "Maybe I ought to go and have a little chat with Pastor Gary."

Two nights later, Pastor Gary Borden and Paul Masterson met after work at the parsonage. The men were good friends, having known each other for more than 30 years. They shared a love of outdoors sports: fishing, hunting, and camping. Once a year, they traveled to the northern woods of Pennsylvania to hunt deer; occasionally they could be found on the banks of the James River, silently standing shoulder to shoulder for an afternoon of what they liked to call "a spiritual retreat." Though not much passed verbally between the two, a deep friendship developed over the course of time and a strong bond of brotherhood formed.

Tonight, the men talked with an intensity and urgency that few people would recognize in them. Together they tackled spiritual questions nagging them for years. Paul revealed his deep desire to do more for Jesus but expressed that his fear of failure held him back and relegated him to a life of passing out bulletins and circulating the collection plate. Pastor Gary divulged a long-held disillusionment with the institution of the church. He secretly considered quitting the ministry altogether on numerous occasions.

"The fire is gone Paul," he confessed. "I feel like now I'm in it for the paycheck and the job security – how horrible does that sound? I'm too old to get back in to the job market. Besides, I don't even know what else I'd do."

By the dim light of the desk lamp in his study, Gary Borden and Paul Masterson worked out their salvation with much fear and trembling. When the mantel clock struck two o' clock in the morning, Paul slid on his coat and shook Gary's hand.

"This is gonna be okay Gary. I think it's the right thing to do. It feels a lot like Jesus."

Lucid dreaming has considerable potential for promoting personal growth and self-development, enhancing self-confidence, improving mental and physical health, facilitating creative problem solving and helping you to progress on the path to self-mastery.

- Stephen LaBerge

Chapter 2

To Dream the Improbable Dream

The sing-song sound of a Sunday school rhyme floats airily in the background. *Here's the church. Here's the steeple. Open the door and see all the people.* It repeats, growing and swelling in both volume and intensity. *Here's the church. Here's the steeple. Open the door and see all the people. Here's the church. Here's the steeple. Open the door and see all the people.* Reaching its crescendo, the song clatters against the bare walls of a darkened sanctuary, echoing through the empty room. But upon a second glance, the room is not empty at all. A lone figure attired in a white

15

undershirt and jeans sits, unmoving, three pews from the front. His head, seemingly bowed in retrospective concentration, lilts to the right, chin resting on chest. A second person, a man, holds a commanding stance on the speaking platform behind a translucent podium. The posture of his form suggests confidence, yet as his hands grip the sides of the podium, his white knuckles reveal a deeper sense of trepidation.

The man at the podium plunges into a speech – a sermon, really – marked with passion. Driving vocal undulations, charismatic gestures, captivating illustrations, and an underlying sincerity seek to engage the audience of one and move him forward to a level of understanding previously unbeknownst to him. As the speech reaches its climactic wave and then slowly recedes into the ripples of conclusion, the speaker notices that the man in the third pew remains unmoved. With an overwhelming sense of confusion and an internal ire moving toward the boiling point, the speaker descends the steps to confront the other man. Coming within steps of the third pew, the speaker quickly realizes that the man is, in fact, sleeping! After being witness to what was arguably the most convincing and moving of sermons, this man remained sound asleep! Appalled at the sleeper's arrogance, the speaker takes hold of the man's shoulders and shakes him, driven by his indignation. As the sleeper's chin pops up from his chest, his eyes flutter open. But instead of the groggy confusion present in those who awake prematurely from sleep, the man's eyes flash with an instant alertness and pointed attentiveness, locking directly on the speaker.

In that moment, the speaker gasps, releasing the sleeper's shoulders and covers his mouth with his right hand. The speaker backs away slowly, unable to release his eyes from the man in the third pew.

It is Jesus, the Christ.

***

Michael Vinings burst from the tangle of blankets covering his body and his bed and found himself gasping for air. He tried to slow his breathing. "In through the nose and out through the mouth," he muttered to himself. His wife Laura, a notoriously sound sleeper, lay peacefully next to him. Michael whispered a "thank you" into the darkness, grateful he did not have to wake her and explain what was happening.

Michael always experienced the same reaction to this dream. Panic.

For the past six months, he had been subjected to this series of events at least once a week – sometimes more. The dream never varied in its story; it was always the same place, the same sermon, the same result. It's just that in his waking, Michael never seemed to be able to put the pieces together. He felt like Nebuchadnezzar staring at the mighty statue, wishing a Daniel would stroll along and explain everything.

Upon waking, Michael also found it difficult to fall back to sleep. Thoughts drifted in and out of his mind, intermingling with the responsibilities and "to-dos" of the next day. After about an hour of this, *that voice* entered his mind and took over.

You're losing members, Michael. Three years in a row there have been slight ticks downward. Most people don't notice while sitting in the worship service, but you get the numbers; they don't. You need to meet the needs of your flock, Michael. You must be doing something wrong. Try a little harder. Reach out to the old, tired, resistant, demanding, and entitled. They want security, comfort, and reassurance. Meet their needs. Work a little harder. Be a little more creative, a little more forward-thinking. Minister to those who push, who want something fresh and new. Provide the enticing, the exciting, the enthusiastic. Use your skills, Michael, your gifts. If you were just a little more talented...

Tonight was no different. At first, Michael tried to assert a positive course of reasoning against the serrated edges of the defeating argument that replayed itself in his head. "Be reasonable, Michael," he thought, "The problem is a demographic change in the community. It's temporary. There is bound to be a bounce soon. You're not doing anything wrong. The problem is the people. This is an established church that we have remade, so to speak. Remember the cycle before when we changed the name, the style, the personality of the church, and it worked? What had been a ten-year slide in attendance and offerings became a four-year uptick."

But these feeble perceptions were no match for the persistence of anxiety, just as hope struggles to dispute what is concrete. Thus, Michael rolled over to begin the endless cycle once more and drifted off into a fitful, restless sleep.

***

Rise and shine. With a classic case of bed head and hair pointing in seven different directions, Michael arose early the next morning. Memories from the night before began to sweep across his mind, but he pushed them aside not wanting to relive the anxiety his unexplained dream continued to cause. Marching on into the shower, Michael prepared for the day ahead.

Out the door with a travel mug filled with coffee which read "Best Freakin' Dad Ever!" Michael eased into his CRV. Cruising through his picket-fenced, tree-lined neighborhood, he ran through a mental check list for the day: respond to Vicky Buskirk's e-mail on the importance of properly laundering the baptismal robes; schedule a meeting with Judy Armstrong to hear about the trials of the prayer shawl ministry; contact Jarrod Bronkowski regarding the leaking ceiling in the men's room; meet with the rest of the staff to touch base and go over Sunday's agenda; prepare the notes for the sermon.

Michael worked hard. He worked long hours. He read a lot of books and went to a fair amount of seminars, some church and some business, to learn the art and science of leadership. A driven pastor, Michael felt proud of the progress he had made during the course of his ministry career. Gifted in time management, he had divisions for each day with a distinct and specified time to study, read, schedule meetings, mentor staff, and interact with leaders in the congregation. Anything less would not be authentically him.

Typically, Michael's days were jam-packed with little breathing room. Today was strangely different. Michael's to-do list for the day felt unusually light. "Maybe I'll even get home in time to catch Taylor's Little League game," he mused.

He pulled into the parking lot five minutes early and stole one last sip of java before entering through the glass doors of the building. Amazingly enough, Patricia already beat him there. Patricia, Michael's stalwart secretary, wore pearls, brooches, and made the most amazing blueberry buckle this side of the Mississippi. She was a master of efficiency and ruled the supply closet with an iron hand. Few knew how attentive and compassionate she was, and she liked it that way. In the office, she was Michael's rock.

"Morning, Patricia," Michael said.

"You're late," she retorted.

"No way, I'm five minutes early today," he responded, a little defensively.

"Five minutes early is as good as ten minutes late. Everyone is here for the meeting. They all came in *early* today and wondered if we could move the meeting up. I looked at your schedule and thought it was a "can-do" so I let them into the conference room.

Hope you don't mind. This should save you some time to work on your sermon today."

No response was needed to acknowledge this change in schedule because Michael knew that once Patricia made a decision there was no going back. "Good, old, efficient Patricia," thought Michael as he smiled to himself and attempted to hide the smirk with his coffee cup.

The weekly staff meeting consisted of going over the highlights and challenges of the week, with each person helping create a punch list for the coming week; there was always open time for staff to offer ideas, insight, and assistance. The team functioned well – professionally and spiritually. They were a tight-knit group of people, and while everyone directed their own areas of ministry, all cared about each other to the extent that they would readily help another member out, even if that meant chipping in on somebody else's work.

Just twenty minutes in, the team covered arts and also care ministries: the in-house benevolence and pastoral connection. The next item on the agenda was a brief review of other ministry areas. As Carol, the children's ministry leader, cleared her throat to launch into her update, it happened. She started to weep. She apologized and Patricia, sitting next to her, reached out and touched her gently. Carol gathered herself but then broke again. The room changed. Everybody became laser focused. A whisper of prayers gently rose from around the table, independent of each other, but very connected to Carol.

No one knew exactly what to do or say. Patricia increased her touch until it became a gathering arm around Carol's shoulders. Jonathan, the worship pastor, asked if he could pray aloud. Carol nodded, unable to speak.

"Father," he prayed, "your daughter is hurting right now. We are her family, her partners, her friends. We want so desperately to help her but we are not You. You can help her and You can use us to do it. We just ask You to invade this room right now. Capture Carol's tears and make them the water with which You nurture the seeds of healing, help, and care for Carol. We offer ourselves and this moment to You right now. Give Carol strength right now to be open where she feels she can share appropriately, and may we listen to her with Your heart open in ours. We pray this in Jesus' name, amen."

The room was quiet. Carol began to apologize again, this time she went on. "Last night, I got home late from one of my ministry meetings. Jerry was still awake... and he was mad," sobs began to choke her once more; she struggled to hold them back. "He just began railing against my work here at church. Basically, he said that I'm not the same, vibrant, God-loving woman I was before I took this position. He questioned what I was doing, who I was really reaching for God. He...he..." she cried without restraint, "he wanted to sleep on the couch..." she trailed off in a wave of tears. After a few moments, Carol stopped and cleared her throat, trying to muster whatever courage and resolve she had left. She continued shakily, "After all of that, I could not sleep. It was hard to admit, but I realized that Jerry was right. I thought about how much I am doing and how little time I have for me and God anymore. Then I began to talk to the Lord and it was hard. What was once so easy is now like I am awkwardly talking to a stranger or a distant relative. I kept seeking God's touch of affirmation on my work but I didn't find it.

Last night, I drilled down two or three levels into my soul and came to some ugly and revealing conclusions. I sit here with you, my closest confidants and friends, and need to repent. I do not want to 'work' for God anymore. I will still work, but I want to work *with* my Father, not *for* an entity, even a Divine entity.

Michael, I don't know how to tell you this, but I have to pull back. I don't want to lose my place of influencing young lives, but I do have to redefine how that happens. I cannot give myself to others to the point where I take myself away from God and from my family.

I feel deeply that you will see more spirituality and fruit if I can make my contributions to the ministry with a new rhythm. I have a plan that requires less hours, fewer meetings, and some handoff to my team. I would like to submit this to you and the elders for consideration, since I know this is not the job description I signed on for. Let me be clear: my request is not negotiable. If you can't agree, I will understand, but I will have to resign, and leave the staff."

A heavy silence blanketed the room. Michael looked around the table at each of his staff members. This was definitely not on the agenda.

Questions rocketed through Michael's mind. How could he gain control of this situation? What was the solution? In a round-about way, Carol's confession suggested that the leadership – the captain at the helm – was steering the ship in the wrong direction. The suggestion, though unintentional, stung. With hundreds of members, thriving programs, and money in the bank, Michael's church exemplified the picture of organizational health. How could it be that in the midst of all this blessing, all this prosperity, they had somehow missed the point? Had he also been guilty of trading working *with* God for the great counterfeit: working *for* God? Michael quickly reigned in these notions. No, this wasn't a leadership issue, this was a Carol issue. The problem lay in her own spiritual growth and development. Her perfectionism led to this. But even though his mind created this solution, it still didn't sit well. This information needed to be processed, thought through and examined. Leaders have to make hard decisions even when it affects friends, right? Carol's terms seemed so rigid; Michael felt backed into a corner.

Like a slow, gray fog, silence continued to cloak the room in solemnity. Around the table, heads remained bowed, no one able to meet another's gaze. Knowing that his next move would set the tone for the rest of the day, Michael deliberately paused before speaking. He led in with a heavy sigh.

"Who else here feels what Carol feels?" One by one, they all looked up. No one said a word.

Michael asked the same question in a different way. "Does anyone want to express what you feel about what Carol has shared, in relation to where you are right now?"

Still, no one said a word.

Carol interjected, "I am sorry. I know there is no good time for this and I did not mean to bring it up. I just couldn't go forward with the status quo in my work. But, I do not feel less called to a place or a group of kids than I did yesterday or last week, or even when I first began. The way I'm doing my job here just isn't working."

Unexpectedly, Jonathan coughed, as if leading into a comment. Michael knew Jonathan to be a goal-oriented leader who made things happen, who got results. Jonathan's confident, take-charge nature impressed Michael the first time he interviewed. So it was with a sense of relief that Michael now directed his attention to the one person at the table who could provide some objective perspective on the situation.

Jonathan began. "I'm not sure how to say this, because I feel like the words I want to say have just appeared to me," he paused, visibly struggling to complete his next series of thoughts. "You all know me; you know how I roll, how I work. I love getting it done and doing it well. When things come together, I feel this sense of accomplishment. I love the applause after worship, the complements…actually, I love being on stage in the spotlight." He hesitated a moment. In the space of an instant, tears began to form at the corners of his eyes and stream down his cheeks. Unabashedly, he continued, "I have been the center of the show, not God. And what is worse…I have relished every moment." He choked out these last words as if the shame of this realization were physically too much for him to swallow.

"I mean, just look at where things stand now," he went on; Michael held his breath. "In *really* seeing things now, I look at all the work we put in to make everything just right for people and wonder if it is worth it. I don't see a church filled with people who are making a difference in our community. I do not see people leading others to Jesus. We pump and pump and pump for people to invite people to come to church, but why? Why aren't we teaching people to take the church away from here? I look at my worship team and I realize I spend hours with them each week – I push them toward perfection. I hammer them with demands and load more and more expectation upon their shoulders," he sobbed. "And yet I never have time to sit, listen, talk, disciple, lead, pastor, or shepherd. Hell,

26

I'm not even *loving* most of them! Oh God," he cried out, "Forgive me!"

Michael sat transfixed at the scene unfolding around him. One by one his staff members poured out confessions of selfishness, waywardness, frustration, disappointment, depression, pride, greed, confusion, and even loss of faith. One by one, the pillars of leadership on which he'd built his church began to crumble, brick by imperfect brick, before his eyes. Anxiety began squeezing his insides. He felt assaulted. The leader, the pastor, the shepherd of souls – was he just a big hoax? Essentially, each person's profession confirmed Michael's inequities and gave proof to his own loss of direction. Unable to wrap his brain around the ruins of all brought forward by his staff, he did the only thing he knew would give him peace. He stepped up to lead.

"Thanks to each of you," he began, "for sharing what was on your heart today." All eyes locked on him as he continued, "To be honest, I'm not sure what to make of it all. I know that when we pour out and pour out in serving people, we all get tired and overwhelmed. We get to those places where we need to take a few steps back, evaluate our commitment to the mission, and make hard decisions sometimes. It seems you all care enough to ask the right questions. Again, thank you."

Michael took a deep breath. This felt better, felt more like control than chaos. He fell back into his trusted leadership strategy: structure. Providing structure meant that no detail got overlooked.

Structure allowed for thoroughness, safety. In essence, Michael began to throw up some steel girders of his own design into the crumbling building.

"I do have a couple of ideas that I think will help us get back on track," he explained. "I want to offer everyone an extra two days off each month. Take those days as a spiritual retreat, for time to reflect and recoup." He barreled on despite the blank stares. "Also, let's begin our staff meetings with a prayer and Scripture reading beginning next week. It will help us stay on track spiritually and give us a chance to share prayer needs."

Despite the fact that his suggestions met with icy silence, he continued on. "Finally, we have to look at the fact that we have had seven new families join in the last quarter and that tells us we are doing what we are here to do, reach the community. So, as tiring as it gets, I am committed to leading you with love and understanding. Just tell me anytime you need a break and we will sit down and make sure you are well taken care of."

With that, Jonathan rose from his seat and gathered up his papers. Without a step of hesitation, he walked past Michael and toward the open conference room door. He grasped the handle, turned for one last look, and slammed it shut…hard.

When eating an elephant take one bite at a time.

-Creighton Abrams

Chapter 3

The Elephant in the Staff Meeting

Michael looked around the room, bewildered at what had just happened. In an effort to diffuse the situation and appease the tensions and frustrations circulating around the room, he now realized he had – most assuredly – made things worse.

The faces of his staff confirmed this feeling. Carol bit her lip and avoided Michael's gaze; Patricia scribbled furiously in her notebook; Brandon, the youth pastor, sat bug-eyed, mouth wide open, staring at the door. Evan, the new intern in the office, shifted in his seat, nervously running his hands along the arms of his chair.

"Well…I…um…," Michael stammered awkwardly. He felt completely ill-equipped to handle the situation before him. The core of his church now lay in complete ruins. Getting anything together for Sunday seemed impossible.

This was not familiar ground for Michael. How suddenly things fell apart; how unprepared he felt to take care of it all. With the abrupt realization that he was on a sinking ship, a feeling of complete helplessness washed over him. Like nothing else he had ever experienced, the recognition of defeat created a vacuum in his soul that systematically began sucking out everything he had once worked so hard to create within himself: confidence, hope, security, capability, respect, responsibility, worthiness, intelligence, optimism, courage, character, and joy. What he once counted as reality – a vibrant church body with an established, charismatic leadership team – now revealed itself to be nothing more than a great pretense. Underneath the polished poise of the staff lived the ugly truth that all these dedicated "church" people (headed by their fearless leader and pastor) – in an effort to create a church deemed successful by the worldly measures of wealth and high attendance – failed to keep focused on honoring God and keeping him at the center of their ministries.

As a result, chaos now reigned.

The weight of it all became too much for Michael. A sour sickening seemed to roll through his insides. The room slipped away before his eyes, and he struggle to maintain his focus. From the vents in the ceiling blew an artificial breeze, and it skimmed the back of Michael's neck making him shiver. Patricia's clicking pen, once a benign background sound, now ricocheted off the panels of the conference room and pounded in Michael's ears. The loss of control, the confusion of it all assaulted his body as much as it did his mind.

Searching for some answer, struggling to regain his footing, Michael recalled a verse of Scripture. Isaiah 41:10 served as a life verse for him during his early years in ministry. Somehow, recently, he had set it aside in his mind, in favor of several new strategies he had picked up at a recent leadership training session. But it came back to him now. As a matter of fact, it pulsated in his mind. Rhythmically beating in time with his breathing, the words of the verse brought a semblance of calm to his mind. *I will strengthen you and help you; I will uphold you with my righteous right hand. I will strengthen you and help you; I will uphold you with my righteous right hand. I will strengthen you and help you; I will uphold you with my righteous right hand.*

Oh the power of the miraculous and God-breathed words in Scripture! Every verse, every story encasing vast recesses of meaning and housing untold treasures of wisdom. While the divine words of direction repeated themselves in his head, Michael sensed an easing in his body. He released his confusion in order to embrace God's direction. Yes, God would strengthen him and help him in this. The Lord's righteous right hand – the hand of blessing, power, and might – would keep Michael from withering in the face of this disaster. Whatever lay ahead, Michael could meet with confidence.

In the span of a few moments of awkward silence, God delivered a life preserver to the captain of this sinking ship. He knew now; he knew how to move forward, or at least how to move forward for the next few minutes. But, ironically, to a man who had his life scheduled and planned into the New Year, this was all he needed.

Humbled by this new perspective, Michael began again. "I'm sorry," he said simply. "I was not trying to belittle your feelings – any of your feelings." Regret encased his heart as he looked at the closed door, wondering where Jonathan had gone and if he would be back. "I wanted to fix it but also be sensitive to Carol and Jonathan and their respective needs for time and space and reflection. I wanted to stay positive in the midst of all this…" he trailed off, momentarily awakened again to his own negligence. "I never thought to stop and pray first," he confessed, almost to himself. "I…we…no, *I* have left the Lord out of my leading."

For the first time during the course of the meeting, Patricia piped up, her arm still encircled protectively around Carol. "Pastor, look, we know you and know you're doing the best you can. Sometimes things get in the way. Life is tough, and when stuff comes at you, it's easy to just hop in there, whip out your tool belt, and get to start fixin' things."

Brandon also contributed, "This isn't just your fault; it's not one person's fault really. We are responsible for our own relationship with God. When it falters, it's not because someone else made that happen. Sure there will be distractions in life. This is part of what I try to teach my kids – you have to make choices, and as a believer, those choices *must* put God first. But that doesn't mean it's easy to do." Brandon looked to each of his colleagues; his manner was sincere, his delivery simple. "Our job as leaders is harder. There is a different standard – even the Bible says that. And," he continued, "there is also a target on our backs. We know that the enemy who seeks to kill and destroy doesn't want strong leadership at the helm of any body of believers. I often think that distraction is one of his most powerful weapons."

At that moment, the door creaked open slowly. From behind its edge appeared a red face - tear-streaked and visibly strained.

"Can I come back in?" asked Jonathan in a rather sheepish way.

Nods of assent and grim smiles bid him welcome.

Head down, Jonathan shifted uneasily from one foot to the other. His hand still on the door knob, he stayed rooted to his spot just inside the room. When he spoke, his voice sounded hoarse, barely above a whisper and decidedly not full of the confident bravado his tone usually took on. "I'm sorry," he began weakly, "I let my emotions control me when I did not get what I thought was going to happen. It's just that," he broke off to consider his next words carefully. "It's just that I feel we all need to address this issue. It's big! I mean, it seems like we're running this church and none of us feels connected to God." As he continued, the passion in his

34

voice swelled and his movements became emphatic. "How ridiculous and scary does that sound? I'm not saying that we're doubting our faith or anything foundational like that, I'm just saying our 'can-do' attitudes have replaced a reliance on the Spirit." Gesturing wildly now Jonathan took a few tentative steps toward his colleagues. With each step, his assurance seemed to grow. Everyone around the table watched as Jonathan transformed before their eyes.

"We want the right things, we know what God wants too, but we've just become so good at what we do and so focused on *successful* results that we've moved away from *depending* on God and seeking out where his Spirit is already working. Like I said, that's a big deal and one that can't be catered to with a couple of days off."

Amazed at how similar Jonathan's realizations were to his own, Michael chimed in, "I'm glad you're back Jonathan, and again, I'm sorry for my reaction. I think deep down I wanted to agree with you all. I wanted to jump on the band wagon of disillusionment, but I was afraid of what you'd think of me." He continued, "I am not energized either. Not that I cannot keep going or doing what I am doing, but I just feel like 'what's the point of it all?' I know how to do my job, organize, speak, teach, and smile but deep inside, just like you, I have frustrations, desires, unmet needs, and a growing discontent that what we are building is not what God asked us to do."

Around the table, tensions eased. Michael could feel it. Everyone could.

As if searching for a safe path in the darkness, Michael went on. "Sitting here after Jonathan left, I had a realization…no, a revelation. For the first time I realized…no, again, I *confess*, that my style of leadership brought us to this place."

A cacophony of "No!" and "Don't go there Michael," attempted to console and reassure, but Michael would have none of it.

"Just hear me out," he said. "I push product and measurable results. In reality, I guess I'm uncomfortable with the unseen because I can't point to it to prove I'm worth the money you're all paying me." He chuckled and smiled feebly. "Seriously, it's much easier to demonstrate the health of the church through offering tallies and the number of new members each month than it is through spiritual growth and freedom from strongholds. Likewise, compassion, generosity, humility, patience…they are all vital characteristics of the Body, but it's hard to include them in the annual budget or write them up for the elders in a monthly report." He breathed a heavy sigh and leaned back in his chair. He suddenly felt as if he had been working for hours. He continued, "Guys, we've just lost our first love." The statement met with emphatic nods and quivering lips.

"And as much as I'm just not sure if another year of business-as-usual will cut it for me, I also don't know how to go about changing course. I am scared I will blow up the church . . . not literally. (Everyone politely laughed.) I wonder if I change, how it will affect the church? And, if I want to change, how do I do it? Will anyone be willing to change with me? What if no one will? The institution of church is really the bedrock of our faith community."

Silent since her initial confession, Carol leaned in, elbows on the table, and said, "So what do we do from here? What's our next step, Pastor?"

Five pairs of eyes rested on Michael. He returned each gaze, raised his shoulders, and gave a helpless shrug.

***

A week after he and Paul Masterson met, Pastor Gary Borden appeared before his elder board. He had requested a special meeting, and had worked with Paul during the time leading up to it to prepare his proposal. After meeting that night, talking and praying into the early hours of the morning, a new course for the direction of the church became clear. Both men felt the presence of the Holy Spirit throughout that evening. Paul, who demonstrated an acute sensitivity to the Spirit's leading that night, affirmed Gary's plan for the church. Now Gary prayed that the Spirit would somehow, miraculously, move in the hearts of the board the way he did in Paul.

"Evening, everyone," Pastor Gary began. "Thanks so much for meeting tonight. I have some things I want to share with you."

Caleb Brass, the head of the elder board, addressed Gary, "Pastor, we always appreciate hearing from you. You have the floor tonight, tell us what's on your mind."

Oddly, Gary felt relaxed as he began to unveil the events leading up to the night. "I want to confess to y'all that I've been feeling…well, a little disheartened lately with the church." Several surprised looks crossed the faces of the board accompanied by a few faces of disapproval. "Now I don't mean this church only," Gary clarified, "but the church at large, the Christian community. I guess I'm just not seeing the life transformation I hoped to see or maybe I'm just getting too gray and have seen it all already." A couple smiles broke across the weathered, more experienced faces on the board. "Anyway, I know I'm not alone in my feelings. I meet with a group of pastors once a month, and this a common feeling among us all. When Jesus left this earth and called on his disciples to carry on his message and bring the gospel into the far corners of the earth, I don't think he had spaghetti dinners and car washes in mind."

Gary surveyed the group to gauge the temperature of the room. Warm. Definitely warm with a trend toward heating up. Assessing each of the faces around the table, Gary could tell that his words struck a chord with some and created discord with others. Still, he continued, "Several weeks ago, our pastor cluster invited a speaker to our meeting: Stuart Moyer. Stu – that's what he wants us

38

to call him – works alongside a team of ministers, most are former pastors, who give their lives and energy to support working pastors who want to live and lead a mission more than they want to administer and manage a church. They call themselves 'reFocusing.'" At this point, Gary clearly captivated each of the members on the board. He wondered if others in the church shared his sense of disillusionment as well.

"What does this Stu guy do then?" questioned Harold Vance, the senior-most individual on the board. Harold attended the church ever since his parents dedicated him at 10 weeks old. He was now 83. Harold loved Jesus and really loved the church…exactly the way it was…back when he was dedicated at 10 weeks old.

Gary turned to respond directly to Harold. "Well, as far as I understand it, Stu and his group help support and encourage pastors to really think about what God wants and how their churches fulfill the Great Commission. Stu finds that most leaders just do not know how to draw strong leadership and direction out of their relationship with God. He says that many pastors feel their relationship with God is more perfunctory and based on ministry than it is personal."

"Is that how you feel Gary?" asked Daphne Davies. Daphne, a compassionate servant among the church body, always asked insightful probing questions and wasn't afraid of messy answers.

"Well, yes, I guess I do…or did," answered Gary, truthfully. "It's just that when Jesus is your job, well, it's easy to lose sight of how he works."

"What do you mean?" The gravelly voice in the corner belonged to Timothy Gerard. Tim owned a bookstore in town and regularly hosted poetry readings and author signings. His connection to individuals in the community provided abundant opportunities to share his faith.

"It's like this," Gary explained, "as a pastor, I don't just have to worry about teaching the Bible. I also need to worry about how the bills get paid, update the church website, show up at every fundraiser, every birthday party, and every church picnic. I also am on call every day at all hours; I welcome babies into the world with a prayer and have the privilege of ushering dear believers out of the world with a verse or a song. Don't get me wrong, I love that stuff, but here's the kicker. I am the one responsible for it all. It's the pastor's job to make sure the whole church is successful and everything goes smoothly. And when it doesn't, well, then it's also the pastor's fault.

And quite honestly, it's impossible, because I can't be the only one – I'm not called to be the only one – doing it all. It's kind of like," he paused, searching his mind for some analogy or brilliant illustration. "It's like being a foreman on a construction site. I'm the guy in charge, but I'm not the one laying the concrete or putting up the walls or shingling the roof. No way that I could get it all done!

40

Yet, if any one of those things goes wrong, it's my head on the chopping block."

"All that responsibility sitting squarely on a man's shoulders wears him down – and can wear down his faith. I love the Lord with all my heart; I believe in the authority of his word, the divinity of his Son, and the power of his Spirit. But I feel like I can't just be his friend. There is too much riding on the idea of God to just settle into developing a real, authentic relationship with God."

The naked candor with which Gary shared drew nothing but an intense, thoughtful silence from those around the table. Unnerving though it was to think that one's pastor didn't have a close relationship with God, the realization of it somehow made Gary seem more like a regular Joe than a Bible superhero. As each person digested what Gary divulged, the atmosphere in the room changed. The charged mood mellowed somewhat, and a feeling of unspoken unity grew in its place.

"So how does Stu and his reFocusing group factor into all that you have shared? Do they just coach you in your thinking or do they go farther than that?" Daphne asked.

Gary said, "There are three things they try to do, but first, you really have to commit to change. When a pastor promises to really seek transformation, the first thing the refocusing group does is listen to pastors who have decided that the ABCs of ministry are not satisfying. The whole Attendance-Buildings-Cash metric doesn't calm the soul.

Second, Stu and the group guide those pastors who really want to engage in the mission of Jesus, to develop people who, in turn, develop people in the way of Jesus. It's the whole idea of disciple-making, except I'm not the only one responsible for it. They believe God has given us insights and tools that are helpful to leading a mission to a community and not just working to produce a Sunday morning gathering. They actually host regional events to introduce these ideas and insights to pastors *and* church leaders, then those people – the pastors and church leaders - can decide whether or not to go it on their own or enlist reFocusing to assist."

"Are you sure this isn't some money-making scheme?" interrupted Harold. Ever vigilant against a bum deal, Harold placed his trust in few people.

"No, it's not a money-making scheme. I don't even think that money changes hands," said. Gary. "They just want to see lasting revival happen. I've seen the results of their efforts, and it's the real thing." He continued on with the final point, "The last thing that reFocusing does is stick with you. They are committed to an ongoing relationship with a pastor on many levels—coaching, mentoring, training a congregation, and facilitating discovery workshops. And that's kind of where I am. I want to sign up. I want to take a select group from church and attend a workshop. I think this is what we need."

Several members of the elder board exchanged glances with one another. Gary wasn't sure where he stood now. He had shared an awful lot; he was pretty sure that some folks wouldn't totally understand where he was coming from and could take his disillusionment the wrong way. But there was nothing he could do about that now. Everything was out in the open – for better or for worse.

Tim was the first to respond. "Gary, I thank you for your honesty and vulnerability. I cannot fathom the courage it must have taken for you to come here tonight and share what you did. I'd be lying if I didn't say that some things surprised me, but I'd also be lying if I said I didn't, at times, feel the same way." Heads bobbed up and down in agreement. "Though I believe that a decision of this magnitude needs bathed in prayer, my initial reaction is to move forward and go for it."

Gary's insides did a little jig.

Robert Benson, a new believer, listened intently to all that was said around the table. His fresh faith led him to consume the Bible like a lion consumes his prey. In short, this young father of four burned fervently for the Lord. Now though, he spoke up shyly, "I like what Pastor said. The more I read my Bible, the more I wonder why all the stuff we do is focused on Christians. I mean, if we're trying to reach the lost, shouldn't we actually try...to get to know...well...people who don't know Jesus? I'm all for it Pastor

Gary, and I'd really love to be a part of the group that gets to go…if prayer confirms that."

"Thank you Rob," Gary said.

"Well, I think we ought to take a vote," the ever-practical Daphne suggested. "I think the proposal on the table is to move forward to pursue the idea of working with reFocusing. I would like to suggest we fast and pray for a period of one week and reconvene to share what we've heard God say. That should then give us the next steps for whatever lies ahead."

Murmurs rose around the table affirming a vote be taken. Daphne called for the vote and it was unanimous, even though Harold seemed to raise a rather reluctant hand.

"Friends," Gary said, moved by the show of support and excited about the potential, "I do believe that God will have some wonderful things in store for us on this journey. I really do."

***

Michael had adjourned the meeting that day in favor of buying some time to think and pray. The staff agreed to spend focused time in prayer for the next steps. Even Evan, the church intern fresh off his sophomore year of college, gave up texting and Facebook for the duration of the week and devoted that time to prayer.

The following week the conference room was once again abuzz with an atmosphere of intensity. But this time, there was a decidedly positive vibe. The church staff took their respective places around the table, and Michael opened up with a passage of Scripture followed by a prayer.

"I want to read from Zechariah 4," he began. "It's the chapter in which the angel is revealing a vision to Zechariah. There is one verse in particular that spoke to me last night as I read the chapter, and I want to share it with you. Verse six says, 'Not by might nor by power, but by my Spirit,' says the LORD Almighty.' It totally hit me," Michael explained. "This whole time, my season of ministry at this church, I've been doing things by *my* might, *my* power. But whatever is going to be accomplished for God, whatever will have a lasting impact on the Kingdom, will be accomplished by *his* Spirit. I just wanted to put that out there. I hope our discussion today can focus in on that. Jonathan, will you pray for us?"

"You bet," Jonathan answered. "Father, let us soak in your Spirit this morning as we look for your way. God, may your Spirit equip us with your courage as we think about new and more sincere ways of living life in this church body. Father God, we confess to you that we've found much satisfaction in our own might and power, but that this way of leading hasn't produced spiritual fruit…it's produced fake, plastic fruit," Jonathan's voice quavered with emotion. "Lord, forgive us and give us a second chance to do this right, to really find ways to join in what you're doing and make

45

a difference for your Kingdom. Open our eyes God, keep our egos in check, and guide us toward you. I humbly ask these things in the mighty, all-powerful name of our Savior, Jesus Christ."

A chorus of "amen" drifted through the room and each person directed their attention to Michael.

***

You see, idealism detached from action is just a dream. But idealism allied with pragmatism, with rolling up your sleeves and making the world bend a bit, is very exciting. It's very real. It's very strong.

– Bono

Chapter 4

Let No One Despise Your Youth[ful] Idealism

Each Sunday, Michael stood on a grand stage with multiple hundreds of pairs of eyes waiting for him to deliver a message that would inspire them and shake them out of the laissez-faire of their suburban lives. And each Sunday, poised confidently on that same stage, Michael spoke the words of God eloquently, at times even passionately, in order to teach and encourage his flock. Today, as a mere five pairs of expectant eyes focused in on him, awaiting the answers and solutions he failed to produce, he felt more terrified than on any Sunday morning.

It was Patricia's voice – a voice whose tones fell somewhere between a school bus driver and a Texas cattle rancher – that broke through the silence of expectation. "Well Pastor," she croaked impatiently, "whatcha' got for us?"

Nothing. Nothing, nothing, nothing, nothing. The words rang out in his head; clanging, clashing together, echoing against the doubts and insecurities that lurked in the deep, shadowy places inside Michael's heart. Though he dutifully fasted during the course of the week and fervently prayed for direction in this problem, God had given Michael nothing. Not one single solution, idea, or strategy. Nothing.

Yet Patricia's question hung heavily there on the table, like a sopping wet quilt from a fraying wash line. Shuffling his papers absentmindedly, Michael tried to buy some time. "Yes Patricia, thank you so much for starting our discussion. I'm eager to hear how the Lord has been speaking to each of you during this week. Our meeting today will no doubt give some great insight…" Michael trailed off as he raised his head from his blank, shuffled papers and gazed at his team. He was doing it again. Unconsciously, but still doing it. Bluffing. Putting on a show. Making nice. Putting up a good front.

Resignedly, Michael sighed. "Well, here goes nothing," he thought. With a sense of defeat creeping up from his gut, he said, "Actually, let me be honest. I don't have anything. I really was praying hard this week, trusting that God would bring something forward to me, but I'm afraid I don't have anything at all. Not one single idea."

Meeting with no response from the rest of the team, he continued on. "I'm sorry about just then." He gestured weakly with his hand, indicating his previous stalling tactic. "I was afraid to tell you I didn't have anything to share. I feel like I've let you guys down."

Michael's eyes shifted downward. He sensed a great disappointment in the room, and it seemed to settle across his shoulders, pushing his head forward in shame. Silence – a familiar presence in the conference room as of late – slunk around the table, drifting in and amongst the team like a fog.

Michael cleared his throat to ask forgiveness again and dismiss the team, when Evan's voice rose up.

"Um, Pastor Michael…um, don't take this the wrong way or anything, but why does God have to give *you* the answers?"

Brandon suppressed an unexpected chortle, which came out as sort of a snort, upon hearing Evan's question. Jonathan and Carol exchanged surprised looks with one another and then swung their eyes toward Michael. Taken slightly aback at this jab, he opened his mouth to speak but was again interrupted by Evan.

"I didn't mean it that way," Evan looked a little injured at the idea that the rest of the team would think he was trying to be disrespectful or critical. "What I'm saying is that God maybe *did* answer your prayers. Maybe he did give a solution to somebody. Maybe it just wasn't you. That still counts, right? There's no rule that says only the pastor can hear from God right?"

Evan's hopeful facial expression met with equally hopeful smiles and nods around the table. Even Michael's taut face relaxed into a knowing smirk as he listened intently to Evan. Encouraged by this affirmation, Evan continued:

"I was fasting and praying too, and the other night, I was reminded of something. A long time ago, when I was just a kid, something happened at our church … or maybe just happened to our pastor. Pastor Gary did a series about how he felt when he hit a wall; not like "crashed" hit a wall, but kind of like had a revelation, hit a wall. He said he came to a fork and took it. My dad and Pastor Gary were pretty good friends, so I asked my dad about it. This road that Pastor Gary hit, well, I remember that it seemed like it was kind of like what we're experiencing now … it ended up that he chose a road not as traveled, or something."

The room laughed.

Brandon then added, "If we take any other road it will be the road less traveled. We are basically a clone of every other contemporary church in our community. You can predict everything that will happen in our services. A few songs, a prayer, an offering and announcements, followed by a message, prayer, and a

"Goodbye, see you next week." And, I am not advocating that changing our style will change anything. But isn't what we are after, or what we are desiring, something deeper, more meaningful?"

Evan patiently waited for Brandon to finish; he leaned in toward the table, an uncharacteristic gleam of assuredness glinting in his eye. When he responded to Brandon, his voice was on the edge of excitement. "But Brandon, there are a lot of different, less traveled paths out there – more than we know. It's just that …" his brow furrowed and his lips pursed as he stopped to try and think of a good illustration. "It's just that those other paths are so hidden, they're really hard to find." Pleased with himself in that college-student kind of way, Evan sat back and folded his hands on his chest. "I think God brought this to my mind because it's going to help our situation."

Jonathan, who had been listening cautiously, urged Evan to continue. "So what did he – Pastor Gary say? What did he do?"

"Well, my pastor told us how he got into a group of pastors who were all feeling the same things. After about a year of, his word was, 'unlearning,' he began to work with our church to start doing some meaningful things outside the building. There was a guy he related to who came in and helped, but the pastor and the elders mostly coached the whole church in changing our face to the community, or, as my mom said, giving our church a face in the community."

Intrigued, Jonathan leaned in. Carol cocked her head to the side and patted her mouth with her index and middle fingers – a position she often took when brainstorming. Patricia rubbed her pearl necklace and chewed her lip. Everyone honed in on Evan's story.

"Our church began to serve at a local elementary school and do whatever the staff needed, and they discovered things they could do for the students. I cannot tell you what all they did but I was about fourteen when this all started, and it's why I am a ministry intern now. I want to be involved with Christians who make a difference. Pastor Gary just got it and his passion was amazing."

Michael, feeling a glimmer of hope rising within him said, "So, Evan, why haven't we heard of this? Who helped him?"

Evan said, "Nobody brings in an intern to teach them."

Smiles emerged all around the table.

"Who did he talk to that helped?" Michael persisted.

Evan responded, "I don't know. That was seven years ago, but I won't forget the name of the guy's ministry because it was odd, not a spiritual name like 'grace' or anything." Again he furrowed his brow in concentration, trying to conjure up the name from the past. Everyone else seemed to hold their collective breath in anticipation.

"ReFocusing!" Evan shouted triumphantly, pumping a fist in the air. "That was it – isn't it weird? ReFocusing is definitely it. And now that I'm thinking about it, what was so neat was the way it happened. Maybe this is what really changed things for me. This whole church transformation made such a difference in my dad's involvement. He was never one of those guys who was going to be asked to be an elder or a leader, so all he could really do was be an usher once a month. He really hated it, but he felt everybody should do something and his spiritual gifts test said he'd be good at passing out bulletins and passing the plate. I think that part of the gift list is in the Gospel of Thomas."

Evan's humor did not get the response he wanted, so he began to just lay out the things his church did. It was amazing that this twenty-one-year-old could so vividly remember details of something that happened more than seven years prior. Being witness to the dramatic change it brought to his home seared the experience into his mind and heart. Seeing the impact of the change on his dad drew Evan's heart toward ministry. God certainly works in complex, miraculous ways.

During the next half-hour, Evan detailed the entire transformation of his home church with fervor and joy. Patricia, sensing the importance of the information, scribbled furiously on her yellowed notepad. Michael jotted down key points, and the others just kept nodding in assent.

When it was all said and done, both Patricia and Michael shared the highlights they recorded which seemed pertinent to their church's particular situation:

Everyone in the church who wanted to was enrolled in a workshop that helped them see a way to make a personal impact on people far from God.

Everyone was given the opportunity to learn how to serve someone they cared about without adding another event to their week.

The church made a history wall that showed them some insights about how they related to the community.

The church membership was energized about doing something focused and tangible for the community around them.

They developed a ministry plan for greater impact as God provided.

They kept doing the first workshops for new people as they came in to the church and the people who were finally ready to get in the new way of church life.

Once Patricia finished reading back some of the elements from Evan's story, Michael leaned back in his chair and felt a smile breaking out across his face. He mused aloud, "So, our least experienced staff member just led us to a moment of significant awareness. Evan, it was so inspiring to see how you remembered the progression and the level of engagement in your church and family. It seems like your church learned how to stop existing only for itself. Amazing."

The reaction from the rest of the group was instantaneous. All around the room, the staff peppered Evan with questions. He did his best to answer, but a lot of, "I don't know, it just worked," popped out of his mouth.

Then he did say, "I'll tell you this; we now serve four schools, have a Habitat for Humanity team, and two or three other things we do on a consistent basis for the city and the county. I think over half the county has been affected by our church and everybody knows we are there to serve. Oh, and we do not talk about this— ever—but we had 350 people when this all started and now we have over twice that many. And, one more thing—we've never invited anyone to church."

An electricity of the Spirit surged through every inch of the room. The atmosphere completely changed from a mere 30 minutes ago. Evan's revelation opened up a flood of ideas from each and every staff member – even the stoic Patricia. The group swirled in discussion for well over an hour, talking about their personal spiritual lives, finding a unique mission serving people outside the church, brainstorming things they felt they could do for different community groups, and prioritizing ways in which they could nurture their own spiritual journeys as well as the journeys of others.

To close the meeting, they prayed corporately, and not a single eye was left dry. Michael dismissed the staff and asked them to take the rest of the day off. Breathless from the exhilaration of it all, he headed back to his office. He desperately needed to make a call.

Each person holds so much power within themselves that needs to be let out. Sometimes they just need a little nudge, a little direction, a little support, a little coaching, and the greatest things can happen.

– Pete Carroll

Chapter 5

Google. Dial. Listen.

Somehow the office felt different.

Standing in the doorway, hand still on the knob, Michael's eyes trailed around the tiny room, soaking in every small detail - the bookshelf full of endless sources of information, the thin trickle of sunlight floating through the window, the piles of paperwork stacked symmetrically on his desk forming a checkerboard of responsibility, the worn, faded edge of his desk chair, evidence of days spent hunched over some problem, trying to work it all out…on his own.

For a brief moment, Michael thought, 'On my own…never again on my own.' With a sense of renewed energy and hope, he plunged into his office ready to tackle the task which the Lord led him to this morning.

Google reFocusing.

Already turned on and booted up, his computer sat humming on the corner of his desk. His fingers flew to the keyboard, and he began an intense search for the reFocusing group. As with most online searches, one link led to another in a spider web of sophisticated convolution. Leads drifted across the screen with every click, and Michael began to grow weary of sifting through all the information. Finally, on a whim, he navigated to a ministry blog written by a man named Stu Moyer. While skimming through a few posts, Michael's eyes hit upon a name: reFocusing. The same name Evan had remembered. Clicking on the light-blue highlighted word brought Michael to a website entitled reFocusing. Jackpot.

"Wooohooo!" Michael shouted. His uncharacteristic outburst drew Patricia to the door. With a scolding and slightly perturbed expression on her face, she asked, "Everything alright in here, Pastor?"

"Definitely," Michael answered, with a grin that looked more like a seventh grade boy caught passing a note in class than a seasoned pastor on the verge of a breakthrough for his church. "I, uh, just found something online that I'd been looking for."

"Online, huh?" Patricia responded, somewhat suspiciously. Though computer-savvy herself, she trusted nothing that came through that magical information highway. "Well, how about you quit your hollerin' and just get back to work then, huh? I, myself, am working on the bulletin and want to get it done. Can't do that with your whooping and all." With that, she slammed the door, leaving Michael to not-so-successfully suppress the smile spreading across his face.

His eyes quickly scanned the site for contact information. A moment later they landed on the "Who We Are" link. After clicking there, he found a link to "Contact Us." With a silent fist pump in celebration (no need to disturb Patricia again), he scribble down the phone number on the page and slid across the floor in his chair over to the phone.

His finger hung for a beat in the air before he dialed. This was it, or could be it. Suddenly a fear gripped him: what if this wasn't it? What if all his hopes for a new start hung on this one phone call and he was completely barking up the wrong tree? What if...?

In that moment, his lips, seemingly independent of his own mind, formed in a whispered prayer. "Lord God, guide my steps here. I want what you want. I'm giving my hopes to you; please lead me in the right direction. Father, I'm tired of being tired. I know there is more to this ministry than what I'm doing. I feel like I'm missing something…maybe missing everything, missing the point. Lord God, help me. Help me see clearly what it is that I need to do. I'm terrified right now that this may not be 'it.' It's clear to me, I don't know the answer. I'm trying to trust you for that right now; Lord I *am* trusting you right now for that. Forgive me for my doubt and fear. Lead me in your ways as I seek to lead this church."

He dialed.

***

"Good afternoon, this is Stu Moyer, how may I bless you today?" A deep, powerful, confident voice met Michael from the other end of the line. To him, the voice sounded familiar, like the voice of a long-time friend.

"Hello? This is Stu Moyer here. How can I help you?" There it came again, and the second greeting jarred Michael out of his stupor. He had not realized he hadn't responded!

"Hello? Yes, hi. Uh, sorry about that. Um, I'm calling for a little information about your company. You see, my church is going through a…transition period…yes, and we're looking for a little support to help us firm up our organizational structure and redefine our ministry vision, and…"

That deep voice gently interrupted, "Hang on there a second, buddy. Before you start throwing all those really impressive words at me, can I get your name?"

Michael's moment of vulnerability before the Lord dissolved the moment Stu answered the phone. He unconsciously slipped back into the guise of his "head pastor" role – professional and polished. In his desire to impress Stu, Michael never offered his name.

"Yes, of course, please accept my apologies," Michael stammered. "My name is Michael Vinings. I pastor Christ Church in a suburb of Dallas. An intern on my staff recommended your organization and…"

"Ministry," Stu interjected. "It's a ministry, Michael. Not a business or a company. We're a ministry, and our mission is people. I'm Stuart Moyer, but please call me Stu."

For whatever reason, this exchange eased Michael's anxieties. A seemingly insignificant invitation of intimacy – calling someone by a nickname – erased the need for pretense. With his mind now set at ease, Michael leaned back in his chair and settled into the conversation, feeling much more like himself. "Thanks, Stu. I'm sorry. I think I'm just a little nervous, or a little eager, or a little…"

"Hungry?" asked Stu.

"Excuse me?" responded Michael.

"Hungry," Stu replied. "Hungry for more of God. Hungry to make a difference in the lives of those who don't know him. Hungry for a relationship with the Creator that reaches down into the depths of your being and fills your spirit like nothing else. Hungry to discover what God really has for you and your church."

"Um…yeah," Michael whispered into the receiver. How did this guy know what Michael was feeling? How could he respond to Michael's thoughts (finish them even!) before Michael formed the words in his mind?

Stu continued, "I know my answer wasn't what you expected. You'd be surprised by how many phone calls I get from pastors just like you expressing these same feelings. It's the truth. Michael Vinings of Dallas, you're not the first pastor who feels that way, and unfortunately, I'm sure you won't be the last. You, and others like you, are the reason we started reFocusing. You see, I am part of a team of ministers, most are former pastors, who give their lives and energy to support pastors who want to live and lead a mission more than they want to administer and manage a church."

Without much thought, Michael blurted out, "How do you do that?"

Instead of giving Michael a firm answer, Stu launched in to a series of very pointed, very revealing questions. "Michael, have you tried a lot of strategies that worked and still felt things were incomplete? Have you heard about and attended a church workshop or seminar, or even read a book that you thought might give you the silver bullet to explode your church and involve your people in ministry? Have you looked at the speakers at one of the conferences and thought, 'How did they make it happen?' Have you hired a ministry coach or growth expert just for your church?"

Michael's head began to spin. 'Yes, yes, yes, and no... but I wanted to.'

"Michael, it is already in you; all of this. Most leaders just do not know how to draw this out of their relationship with God. In fact, we find that many pastors feel their relationship with God is more perfunctory and based on ministry than it is personal."

On the other end of the line, tears welled up in Michael's eyes. It was the first time someone gave voice to all the unspoken fears and frustrations Michael had experienced for years. Every doubt and worry that plagued him, every failure and inadequacy he suffered as a pastor, every hang-up, stronghold, and weakness somehow became undressed and exposed from the other end of the telephone line. Michael always imagined this moment to be incredibly humiliating which is why, for so many years, he pushed these feelings aside and just soldiered through. But now, knowing that he was not the only one to feel this way, now he just felt...free.

"Michael, are you there? Michael?" Again Stu's voice rocked Michael out of his reverie and back into the present.

"Yes, I'm here. I'm sorry. I was just…you just said so many things that I…"

"Struggle with," Stu finished.

"Yes," Michael answered.

"You are not alone Michael," Stu responded. "I am really getting a sense here from the Spirit that this is an important connection. I'd like to continue talking with you, Michael. Right now, I have a meeting that I must attend, but I'd like to call you back when that ends. Would you be willing to give me your number?"

Michael was willing.

***

Three hours later, the phone rang. Michael took an early lunch and then a walk to pray and clear his head. Once more refreshed from spending time in God's presence, he sat by the phone, like a teen-aged girl waiting for her crush to call. The phone rang.

"This is Michael Vinings," he answered.

"Michael, hi, it's Stu. I'm so sorry it's taken me so long. We just had some intense things to work out."

"No problem. Trust me, I know how staff meetings and business meetings can be here at church. I can't imagine tackling those things on a larger scale with your company...uh, ministry."

A soft chuckle bubbled up on the other end of the line. "Oh, Michael, it wasn't actually a staff meeting or a business meeting. It was a prayer meeting."

Though Stu couldn't see it, Michael's mouth fell open in unbelief. A prayer meeting? A three-hour long prayer meeting? At work?

Stu continued, "We make it a point to meet weekly to pray together. We decided early on that since the source of all we have to give comes from God and his Spirit, we'd better stay connected and bring everything to them. It's amazing the ways in which God moves when you give him that authority."

"Yeah, right, I know," Michael responded half-heartedly.

"So, where were we Michael Vinings of Christ Church in Dallas?"

Michael focused back in on the conversation, recalling their first discussion three hours prior. "Well, I think we were kind of forging some kind of relationship. You said that you sensed the Spirit directing a connection...but, if it's all the same to you, Stu, I'd like to hear a little more about your ministry and what exactly you do. I mean, I've heard a lot of people promise a lot of things over the years in ministry. I've read hundreds of books and attended scores of seminars that all say basically the same thing: Follow these steps and everything will turn out perfectly, just the way you want it. To be honest Stu, I think that's been a bunch of bunk. I've done it. I've followed the directions, stood at attention, and although from the outside many would say my church is thriving, from the inside, it's diseased and falling apart."

Michael then began to relate the still-fresh encounter in staff meeting. He began to share all the gory details about Carol's confession, Jonathan's frustration, and Evan's solution. With candid specificity and humble honesty, he communicated his own worries, fears, and anxieties, expressing things that he had never vocalized to anyone else. For his part, Stu listened, silent on the other side of the phone save for an occasional, "Hmmm," or "I see." Michael even shared his mismanagement of the situation – open and vulnerable about his own flaws, needing to "fix" the problem. Finally, he recounted Evan's story and how energized they all felt after hearing about the transformation that his church had experienced. "And so," he concluded, "I picked up the phone and called you."

"Michael," Stu responded in a deliberate, reflective tone, "I do believe the Lord has led you to this point. It sounds like you've really been broken down over the last several days. This is just where he wants you: humbled and ready to admit that you need him if you are going to move forward at all. Sometimes we get so good at the things we do, we forget to ask for the guidance and help of the Lord." He paused and a sense of peace passed through the line.

"I want to help you. I think reFocusing can help you, but there are some things I want you to know before we get started."

Michael just nodded on the other end.

"First," said Stu, "let me tell you more about what we do. We listen to pastors who have decided that the ABCs of ministry are not satisfying. The whole Attendance-Buildings-Cash metric doesn't calm the soul.

"Second, we are open to those pastors who desire an authentic, meaningful pursuit of the mission of Jesus, pastors who want to develop people who, in turn, develop people in the way of Jesus. We believe God has given us insights and tools that are helpful to leading a mission to a community and not just working to produce a Sunday morning gathering. We host regional events to introduce these ideas and insights to pastors and church leaders, then they can decide whether or not to go it on their own or enlist us to assist.

"Third, we are committed to an ongoing relationship with a pastor on many levels—coaching, mentoring, and training their congregation and facilitating our discovery workshops. Interestingly enough," he continued, "we'll be hosting a three-day event in Dallas in about two weeks."

In his office, Michael brightened, "Okay, where do I sign up?"

Stu smiled to himself and answered, "It's not that simple. We need to help you know if you are willing and ready, not just willing *or* ready. Too many pastors get excited and jump on a bandwagon thinking they can hear and reproduce something like it was a program they bought on the internet. You even mentioned it before: just follow the directions and everything will work out perfectly. God does not work in an assembly line fashion. He is not in the business of mass-producing churches. Each unique church body has its own distinctive ministry. It is created and designed to meet a special purpose. It shouldn't look like every other church out there. It needs to seek God and discover His plan for them.

"Likewise," he went on, "our reFocusing process isn't like that. We don't hand out band-aids. We want to get to the heart of the problem. Our change comes from the inside out. As organizational experts say, 'unless the paradigm at the heart of the culture is changed, there will be no lasting change.'" Stu then asked, "What do you know about the missional conversation going on?"

Michael responded transparently, "Not much. I hear that word tossed around a bit. One of the pastors I meet with regularly in my consortium has been doing some reading on it."

Stu expanded. "For most of the last decade, there has been a growing sentiment that the church has lost much of its original charge to be world changers by producing disciples. As a matter of fact, George Barna and others have documented the growing similarities between secular people and Christian people. The distinction is just not as prominent anymore – in our lifestyle, choices, beliefs, concerns, or worldview.

"There have been a few, let's call them missiologists, who have studied periods in history when the church flourished and people forged a great faith that had an unmistakable impact on the culture around it. Two of these men, Michael Frost and Alan Hirsch, wrote a book titled *The Shaping of Things to Come*. In it, they discuss the mission, spirituality, and structure of the movement-born church – a church that exists to serve, develop, and deploy, rather than a maintenance-laden church that collects, contains, and offers education. The missional church is centered on the life and rhythm of Jesus, and not the institution and tradition of the various doctrinal sects, denominations, and structures of hierarchy we are so accustomed to."

As Stu talked, Michael felt like he was getting inside information. Stu also recommended the books *The Forgotten Ways* by Alan Hirsch and *The Shaping of Things to Come* by Hirsch and Michael Frost. He also recommended *Postmodern Pilgrim* and *I Am a Follower* by Leonard Sweet, *On The Verge* by Alan Hirsch and Dave Ferguson, *Missional Renaissance* by Reggie McNeal and others that Michael would have to ask for again later. With a divine hunger for more understanding springing up inside Michael, he decided to make these first books a top reading priority. A sensation of excitement bloomed inside him; Michael felt like he had been awakened by his dad before sunrise to go on an unknown adventure, but one that had no specific definition or outcome. Stu said there was more but that he'd wait and not pile too much on right now. With a renewed sense of enthusiasm, Michael looked forward to the moments, days, weeks, and months ahead.

The sound of Stu's voice broke in to Michael's golden cloud of anticipation. "Here's what I'd like you to do, Michael. First, decide if *you* are ready to live as a missionary to the people in your life. If you are, *then* we can talk about leading your congregation to live 'on mission' for Christ. Second, talk with your staff and some of your trusted leaders and share your feelings with them. It seems like your staff is on board, but you may need more lay leaders as well. Ask if they are supportive of you getting this developmental experience. Finally, talk to a few peers and share your feelings. See if there might be a partnership that can be built so that you are not alone on this journey. If after all that you still feel like this is for you, then call me back."

Michael knew that checking in with others and building a network of support was vital, but he knew – without a doubt – what he wanted to do. Inside, once again, he felt an affirming sense of confidence: not only did he *want* to do this, but it was the *right* thing to do. As the golden cloud of excitement dissipated, a solid, concrete idea settled into his mind. For the first time, Michael felt as though

God delivered to him a clear directive: Go and be a force in your community. This was the answer to the prayer Michael whispered earlier in the day. Instantaneously, like the moment a room is illuminated by a flick of the light switch, Michael realized that "church" is not just for churchgoers. Spending so much time catering to those who claim to already know the Lord diluted the time, resources, and ability to reach those who do not know Jesus. For so many years, he had been preaching to the choir, so to speak.

A spark within Michael ignited something in that moment, and that "something" began to burn. This was it. This was what had been missing; this piece felt like it could complete the puzzle that had been gathering dust, neglected, on the table. With renewed calling, Michael recognized his heart's hidden desire. Reaching out to those who did not know Jesus was his purpose all along, but he had gotten side-tracked with the "business" of ministry. He closed his eyes and exhaled. "Thank you Lord," he whispered into the receiver.

"What was that Michael?" Stu questioned.

"That seems doable, Stu," he answered.

***

*We cannot solve our problems with the same thinking
we used when we created them.*

–Albert Einstein

Chapter 6

reFocusing, One Frame at a Time

For the next few months, Michael's days ran differently.

The first step in Michael's reFocusing journey revolved around asking for the support of his staff and elder board. Before meeting with these folks, Michael spent two full days devoted to prayer and listening. Michael's first obstacle in this was Patricia. She could not, for the life of her, understand why Michael wanted to take two vacation days to pray. Couldn't he just do that in his office?

Patricia's resistance forced Michael to articulate the change that was taking place in him. And though he found it tough to persuade Patricia, after an open, honest conversation, she became surprisingly compassionate and receptive.

The next hurdle came when he addressed his elder board. Comprised of leaders and long-standing members of the congregation, many of the elders balked at the idea of changing things up. Some found Michael's assessment of their church as mainly focused on itself, instead of genuinely reaching out to the community, to be arrogant, misguided, and unbiblical. And these same folks did not hold back their perceptions. Yet others spoke to feeling the same way as Michael did, and encouraged him to move forward. In the end, though two members left the church over this impasse, Michael received the blessing of his elder board to do whatever he felt necessary to move the church closer toward God's vision for it. They even went so far as to pledge regular prayer support for Michael, and he agreed to update them frequently on what he heard from God and learned from Stu.

As for his staff, they unanimously and enthusiastically supported him. They also couldn't wait to hear about what he was learning. Thus, Michael implemented a weekly prayer and discussion time for the staff. He also mandated one day a month as "freedom day," which was to be used (in whatever way the participant saw fit) for personal reflection and prayer.

Michael lived in a parallel transition—one that would depend on more personal responsibility than perfunctory regimen. He sensed God coaxing him into a different rhythm of life and leadership. He began to read from a different mindset, listen from a different paradigm, and see from a different perspective.

In addition to forging stronger spiritual connections with those in leadership at his church, Michael also talked with Stu every few days. Their conversations revolved mostly around questions; Stu possessed an amazing gift to awaken Michael to new concepts by simply posing a thoughtful question. Little by little, and sometimes in ways he didn't quite understand, Michael's thinking began to shift.

The extent of Michael's transformation became most evident during an afternoon pastors' meeting over lunch. As a result of speaking with Stu, Michael opted out of his former consortium of clergy and instead invited David Billings—the pastor who nurtured a keen interest in missional churches—to meet with him regularly. Both men had since forged not only a relationship with each other, but with Stu Moyer as well. They found much common ground, and enjoyed talking through their latest discoveries.

Today, the men lunched at an outdoor café. The sun shone brightly and the air felt distinctly crisp. Seated underneath a neat blue and white umbrella, they fell quickly and easily into conversation. While David munched on a pile of french fries, Michael shared, "I feel like my entire ministry was formed around building a stellar organization and now my feeling is that, going forward, I want to be about building stellar people—in the image and likeness of Jesus."

Taking time and courtesy to swallow the fistful of fries he stuck in his mouth (David's wife cooked exclusively healthy meals – whole food, organic, no junk; David looked forward to meetings with Michael both for the conversation and the freedom to enjoy some good fries), David answered, "I know that you mean. I just finished Leonard Sweet's book, *I Am a Follower*; the conflict of interest he described between the pastor-as-CEO verses an actual follower of Christ seemed so obvious, I wondered how I had missed it all these years." Like Michael, David pastored a financially successful church. A denominational superpower, his church boasted more than 1000 members, ran a thriving daycare center, and recently opened a homeless shelter in an economically depressed area of Dallas. Yet with all that, David felt that he wasn't seeing evidence that his church members were interested in growing a deeper relationship with God. In fact, he felt like the same could be said about himself.

Michael, meanwhile, sucked down a chocolate milk shake and responded to David. "I read that book too. I love Sweet! In some dynamic way, he is able to draw a distinction between the secular pattern that now seems to be the norm in churches and the Scriptural design that Jesus advertised in Matthew 20 when He declared: "You know that the rulers of the heathen lord it over them and that their great ones have absolute power? But it must not be so among you. No, whoever among you wants to be great must become the servant of you all, and if he wants to be first among you he must be your slave—just as the Son of Man has not come to be served but to serve, and to give his life to set many others free." After reading that, I realized I had bought into an authoritarian approach to leadership that was rooted in a position and not a spirit posture. It was the whole 'command-and-control' approach."

David nodded earnestly as he swiped a lone fry through a pool of ketchup. His friendship served as a great source of encouragement to Michael. Meeting a like-minded person in ministry felt truly affirming to him. During these last few months, David had become a very close confidant. Taking another sip of his milkshake, Michael continued, growing in both gusto and volume. "Don't misunderstand me, David; I don't mean to say that efficiently running a church is evil. I mean, one of the gifts of the Spirit is administration. But, I just realized, Jesus had made it abundantly clear this was not to be *my* pattern as a godly leader. I was to lead by following Jesus' example.

"In fact, one quote that influenced me powerfully is this: "Following is the most underrated form of leadership in existence." Totally blew my mind! In essence, Jesus did not make any sweeping, autocratic, leadership decisions for others to follow. His leadership was completely understood in the context that He was emulating, patterning after, and obeying the Father."

"Right!" David said, as he licked his fingers, removing the last satisfying remnants of grease. He relished his recent bond with Michael. He found Michael to be innovative and fresh without being superficial. Michael seemed to display a genuine, passionate desire to pursue God; David valued his ravenous appetite for solid teaching and gleaned a lot out of their conversations. David's wife called them "kindred spirits;" David just thought they were good buds. And as such, he felt completely comfortable sharing his own journey with Michael. "Seriously," David continued once his fingers were clean, "Jesus did not come up with a vision and then strategize how his leaders should carry it out. He didn't designate each disciple to a specific area of ministry after giving them a spiritual gifts test or something. Jesus obeyed a preordained mission and modeled how to be an influencer and carry the mission forward by following his mandated objectives: fellowship with the Father, sense and seek the Father, understand what the Father wants to accomplish, express this to others by activity and purpose, and then live accordingly. There are no institutional or structural objectives; only godly desires that shape obedient living.

"There was another quote I wanted to share from Len Sweet," David said. He wiped the remaining fry oil onto his khaki shorts and grabbed a book out of his laptop bag. "I read this the other night and just had to underline it so that I could find it again when we met. I stink at remembering stuff like this." He thumbed through the pages of the well-worn paperback. "Ah-ha! Here it is. Listen to this." He read: "'The cry for leadership is deafening amid our social disintegration, our moral disorientation. We have come to believe that we have a leadership crisis while all along we have been in a drought of discipleship. The Jesus paradox is that only Christians lead by following." How about that?"

"Do you know what that made me think?" David asked. Michael just shook his head. His attention was completely rapt; he was leaning on his elbows, his eyes sparkling with eagerness.

"That one small quote made me think that I was a pastor and leader in the greatest social entity on earth—the church—and I was leading like I was the president of a corporation." It was David's turn to shake his head, this time with an air of disgust. "I was far from the pattern, personality, and presence of my stated leader, Jesus. I was attempting to accomplish what I had defined as the mission of God, apart from the pattern and model that he, himself, set forth.

I had the notion that I could simply study, pray, and pattern myself after 'successful' ministers. Why did *I* cling to 'command-and-control' leadership? How did I miss the impact on those following me? Why had I not noticed how willing Jesus was to follow his Father? I did not have an answer to these questions. I felt like Abram leaving Ur. I knew I had to follow, but I had no idea where I would end up."

"That's exactly how I felt before I met Stu and started talking with him," Michael chimed in. "All these questions…it now seems so obvious and so clear. At first, I felt like an idiot for not recognizing it sooner."

"All in God's time, Brother," David replied.

"But here's another thing," Michael confessed, his tone more subdued, his head bowed over his empty plate. "It was about me, too. And I didn't get that at first, maybe I didn't want to."

"What do you mean?" asked David.

"I mean, if I'm to be completely honest with myself, I loved being the center of attention at church. I was revered for my words and presence. I dressed in the latest impressive threads, and stood front and center as the voice of authority. I was flanked by elders and deacons who were there to carry out my vision. The way I represented Jesus was so pretentious! Not long after meeting with Stu, I was sitting in my office looking through some catalogue or something, and I saw the famous image of Jesus at the Last Supper. Then something went off in my brain, and I immediately began to think of his journey to the cross. Jesus, headed to death, was humble, and did not use his position or power as God to avert his ultimate service on the cross. He didn't demand the best, latest. He did not demand special treatment or require some level of compensation for his service. He had the power of the universe at his fingertips, and yet..." Michael's voice caught, and he sounded strained as he continued, "I don't know...it just struck a chord in me. Who do I think I am?"

Both men sat in silence for several moments.

"So, when will you talk to Stu next?" asked David.

"I don't know," answered Michael. "We caught up on Tuesday, and he said he'd sent me something in the mail. It should be here today or tomorrow, I guess."

"Sent you something in the mail?" questioned David. "Like, snail mail? What could it be that he didn't just e-mail it to you?"

"Who knows," responded Michael. "You know how Stu can be," he said with a slight grin.

"Yeah," said David, as he lifted his hand to catch the eye of their waiter. The young man, clad in black from head to toe, scurried over to the table.

"May I help you sir?" he asked politely.

"Yes," smiled David. "I'd like another order of fries."

***

The package came the day after Michael met with David. Patricia set it on his desk as she did all his mail. A smile curled on Michael's lips as he noticed the corner of the package slightly lifted. Obviously, Patricia felt curious about the package as well, but then perhaps, thought better of opening it. Michael grabbed an opener from his top desk draw and proceeded to tear into the package. He opened it and found a hand-written note from Stu. It read:

Dear Michael,

Enclosed you'll find a little something for you while we continue on our journey together. Additionally, you'll find our coaching agreement. Please take some time to read through it. Call me with your questions. I'm off for a bit and will return Wednesday.

With joy,

Stu

Sifting through the information in the package, Michael came across a coaching agreement from Stu. They had discussed this covenant recently; it was at this time that Michael looked into Stu's organization in greater detail. He learned that Stu doesn't just accept anyone. First, a rapport and connection have to be established. Second, because he is with a larger ministry, he has accountability and a team he works with to keep him training and progressing.

Finally, Michael discovered that reFocusing had existed for more than fifteen years and that CRM, their ministry organization, was a collection of four hundred mission-oriented people around the world. Their sole purpose was to support the development of leaders who were intentional about becoming missionaries in their context and community, rather than building an institution. These many discoveries solidified reFocusing's legitimacy in ministry.

ReFocusing was indeed a well-researched and comprehensive process that challenged pastors and leaders to embrace a lifestyle of mission and discipling others.

Along with some other paper work, the package also contained a beautiful leather journal. Opening its soft cocoa-colored cover, Michael fingered the thin pages. He smiled knowingly. Stu hinted that he would be sending Michael something special. "You're going to need something to help you keep track of all you're learning," he had said.

And Michael had learned so much! He often sat in his office, almost dumbfounded at the ways in which he used to lead. Now Michael actively charted a course of movement for his own life and leadership. Sometimes a week was not enough to implement his discoveries or fully realize them; Michael always felt like he needed more time to reiterate, rehearse, and replay the new areas of personal change.

One of the biggest changes Michael began to implement was to create time in his schedule to intentionally develop relationships with people who didn't know God. Until this time, his closest friends had all been from the church world—either church members, lifelong friends, or ministry colleagues. Those were the people he invited to his house, went to concerts and sporting events with, or traveled and enjoyed life with. Now, Michael sensed a deep challenge to change his old rhythm and construct margin for extending relationship and to consider how his time could be better used to share the heart of Jesus.

Of course, this path of embracing non-Christians necessitated a hard look at Michael's prejudices. Stu brilliantly dug (with an uncanny gentleness) into Michael's preconceptions about "sinners" and how he related to them. It seemed like all his personal history—his upbringing, seminary training, and experience as a minister—had actually conditioned him to follow an unwritten "script" in his interactions with unbelievers. Instead of authentically engaging in meaningful, interested, relationship-building, Michael often set off an internal timer; one which ticked away the minutes toward making an unbeliever into a believer. In essence, Michael's only desire in creating relationships with those outside the church was to turn that person into a believer. And while that, in and of itself, was not a negative (after all, God calls believers to share his gospel with those who don't know), Michael's motivation was purely self-seeking. Ironically, his "script" somehow missed the entire heart of God for people. Through reflection and discussion with Stu, Michael redefined "evangelism." Evangelizing was transformed from a meager transfer of information necessary to conduct a mental transaction, to an intentional developing of genuine friendship stemming from a love for Christ, instead of a professional obligation.

But that was only one of the arenas where Michael discovered self-change. He learned how to say "yes" to the important and "no" to the unnecessary. He learned how to include family in his personal mission rhythm. He learned how to pastor smarter, not longer. He learned how to appreciate pushback on his leadership and understand different perspectives.

Michael looked up from the journal once more. Considering all that God had awakened inside him already, it was hard to believe that there was more he could reveal. Stu was right, Michael did need to take time to record it all—for the honor and glory of the power of God. This would be Michael's Ebenezer, his stone altar of remembrance. Picking up a pen from his desk, he scribbled:

> Praise God for his goodness and faithfulness! He is the master of all creation and change! I cannot believe how much he has taught to me in these few months – more than I ever learned in seminary! These lessons haven't been easy. In fact, in the coaching calls with Stu, there were times when I was frustrated, angry, beside myself, and at a loss for words. But the grace I receive, both from Stu and from God, is empowering in the very place of weakness. This change has been relational. In moments of pure joy, I feel that God is so happy for me to be engaging with him and not simply employing the code of ministry, morality, or mechanisms that so frequently had framed my life.
>
> I always knew I was related to God, but now I'm feeling like I am in a relationship with God. There is such a difference! In my coaching with Stu, I am beginning to feel that I can honestly be honest. We deal with failings and missteps, but in a way that is discipline oriented and not punitive. Discussions center around having pure motives. That, in itself, is a change for me! While, previously, I did not consciously view building the church in terms of attendance, income, and programs as something selfish, I now realize that my ego rose or fell based on these factors. That was a red flag of the reddest proportions.

> Now, there is nothing wrong with numbers; the Bible reports them, records them, and recognizes them in many ways. However, when my sense of well-being vacillates with our numbers... well, that just destroys the way I relate to God's purpose and pleasure in me.

Michael paused to think, reflecting on what else he gleaned during his time with Stu. During his intermission from writing, he gazed out the window and watched a violently orange sun begin to sink in the sky. He had been in his office for hours! He needed to finish up and get home. He finished the debut entry in his journal before leaving:

> Each new discovery leads me in new directions in my walk with God and my walk as a leader. Now, I find myself much more concerned with how I live out the mission of Jesus away from the church; I'm more aware of people far from God. I feel valuable in an entirely different way. Outside circumstances, such as acceptance or rejection, great attendance or offerings, and pats on the back from parishioners and colleagues, aren't as influential as they were a few months ago. I feel more cerebral and spiritually inclined. I also notice I am losing the sense that I am working for God, and seeking his approval. I now wake up feeling I am working with God with the confidence that I am already approved. Now, that was a difference. I don't remember how it happened, but I'll never forget when it began.

Satisfied, Michael tenderly closed the journal and tucked it into the outside pocket of his laptop bag. He headed home for the night, and for the first time in years of ministry, he couldn't wait to get back in the office the next day.

***

"Stu Moyer speaking; how may I help you?"

"Hey Stu, its Michael. I wanted to touch base with you after the elder meeting. Things didn't go as smoothly as I planned. I encountered a small faction of folks opposing the lunch program. I couldn't believe it. I totally thought everyone was on board! They were all so supportive of some of the other stuff. And I couldn't believe…"

Stu broke in before Michael's tirade gathered too much steam. "Michael, remember our discussion on fruit a few weeks ago? How "fruit" is the result of some activity that is natural and not an engineered process?" Michael bit his lip and just sort of grunted into the receiver. "Well," Stu continued, "do you also remember that when you are evaluating yourself you need to use the criteria that God presides over?" More mumbling over the line. "Michael," Stu said in a firm, no-nonsense sort of voice, "Michael, this is the old you taking over here. Step back and re-evaluate. What are you not seeing? What is God asking? How have you been relating to him?"

Michael took a deep breath. He talked through some of his frustrations with Stu. Stu listened carefully and asked clarifying questions. Then together, they mapped out a plan to help Michael discover and evaluate what he thought really impacted the ability to move forward in this particular situation. Michael emerged from the brief conversation with an awareness of what needed to change, and with a series of intentional actions to effect and anchor that change. Aside from feeling better about the entire situation, Michael felt more physically relaxed.

"Thanks, Stu. I missed the ball on that one. I appreciate you talking me down there."

"No problem, Michael. I'm glad you called. I actually had a conversation with you on my morning agenda. I wanted to ask you something."

"You bet, Stu. What do you need?"

"I don't really need anything," Stu replied. "But I did want to invite you to attend one of our Awaken and Activate workshops. Two weeks from now, I'm planning on being in Dallas. I'd love for you to join us. I think you're ready. I also have someone I'd like you to meet."

Intrigued and flattered that Stu deemed him ready to progress even further, Michael nearly jumped through the phone. "Thanks so much for the invitation Stu! I'd love to come. Who do you want me to meet?"

But Stu didn't answer Michael's question. Instead he simply said, "Super. I'll have Judy, my assistant, send you the link for the registration form. Be sure to fill it out and send it back in the next few days—the workshop is filling up fast. Sorry Michael, but I have to go; I'll see you in a couple weeks." And with that, Stu ended the call.

When we are no longer able to change a situation - we are challenged to change ourselves.

−Viktor Frankl

Chapter 7

Shift to Change

Driving down the four-lane highway headed to his first Awaken and Activate workshop, Michael felt a little giddy. He had taken the day off as one of his prayer and reflection days and trekked up to White Rock Lake, just a bit north of Dallas. One of his favorite spots—and arguably one of the prettiest places in the city—he circled the lake for hours, praying and listening. It was during this time that Michael could have sworn he felt the Lord's growing excitement for him! Silly as it may sound, during his prayer walk, he felt such anticipation about the workshop that his body fairly trembled.

Not the least of his excitement grew out of the fact that he would have the opportunity to meet Stu Moyer face-to-face. He had yet to shake the hand of the man with whom he had shared innumerable private thoughts and dreams, qualms and woes, flaws and shortcomings. And while the pragmatic side of Michael warned, "Don't get your hopes up here. It could be just another weekend conference, a big pep rally," the spiritual side which had developed deep roots over these many months of mentoring sensed that this event could prove to be one of the hinges that moved Michael's life and leadership from an event-based, Sunday-focused rhythm to one of mission and engagement.

Michael arrived that morning at a church similar to his own, about fifty miles away. He walked through two ornate doors and into a small lobby where about ten people gathered loosely around a few tables piled with refreshments. Michael scanned the room, though he didn't quite know what or whom he was looking for. Then, from the corner of the room housing the coffee bar, he heard that unmistakable deep voice.

"Michael!" called Stu, walking toward him with arms outstretched. Clearly not a hand-shake kind of guy, Stu embraced Michael in an enveloping bear hug. Squeezed tight, Michael managed only a choked, "S-Stu?"

"So thrilled that you could make it!" And his smile plainly showed the truth of his statement. "How was the drive? Can I get you some coffee?"

"Do you speak exclusively in questions?" teased Michael, as the two men walked together toward the coffee bar.

Stu burst out laughing. Michael could not remember having ever heard him laugh before. "Oh Michael, this is just so great. Hey, I have someone here who I want you to meet."

Stu extended his arm toward the table with the cheese and crackers and gave a little waving motion with his hand. Out from behind a group of three men emerged an older gentleman with graying temples and a thick beard. The creases at the corners of his eyes bore evidence of a lifetime of joy and his ample midsection proved the culinary mastery his wife of 41 years possessed. He ambled over toward the two men, refreshment plate in hand and piled high with a number of breads and cheeses.

"Michael Vinings of Dallas, Texas," announced Stu with a show of grand staging, "I would very much like you to meet Gary Borden of Winchester, Virginia."

At first, Michael couldn't place the name. He smiled politely, if not vaguely, trying to rack his brain for the connection. As he mentally processed the face, the man—Gary—gripped his hand and shook it saying, "It's so nice to meet you. I'm so glad that our Evan landed in such a wonderful church as yours. It's so exciting to see our young kids following the Lord."

Evan! Of course! Pastor Gary! Immediately, Michael's smile widened as he exchanged the greeting. "The pleasure is truly mine,

Pastor Gary. You're basically the whole reason I'm here in the first place!" Then with a change to an intense, personal sincerity, Michael added, "Truly Gary, thank you for your courage. This has changed my life." His eyes misted over, his hand releasing Gary's.

"I thought it would be great if you two gentlemen got to know one another this weekend," offered Stu. "I know that you come from different backgrounds, but I thought you would have a lot to share. Michael, Gary is your unofficial host for the week. If you have any questions—and I'm not available—please feel free to connect with him. Now will you excuse me?"

With that, Stu began circulating around the room, greeting participants and introducing himself to others. There were two other colleagues with Stu, and they would share the facilitating responsibilities for the workshop. Gary and Michael exchanged some personal anecdotes and talked quite a bit about Evan. Their common desire to build an authentic relationship with God and encourage others to do the same created an instant foundation for friendship. Minutes after meeting, they chuckled heartily, sharing stories of finicky parishioners and embarrassing moments in the pulpit. It was in the midst of this banter that all the participants were invited into the conference room for the first session of the experience.

The workshop proved to be different than any Michael had previously attended. For three hours that first morning, he created a snapshot of his life from childhood to the present. Michael identified the people, places, events, and experiences he deemed significant and important in God's shaping of his life. He then assembled these divergent pieces into an ordered and comprehensive timeline. It was the first time Michael stepped outside of himself and objectively studied all that influenced him over a lifetime. It was fascinating.

This Awaken portion of the workshop provided an opportunity for Michael to genuinely explore and digest his role as a divinely formed follower of Jesus. Within another day, after two more three-hour sessions, he created a "Personal Calling Statement." This piece best described how he felt God created him to be part of the reconciliation process in his world. It included three elements: biblically based identity (Who am I in God's eyes?), important values, and personal impact (How can I reach those who don't know God?).

Both the Timeline and the Personal Calling Statement afforded Michael a wealth and depth of insight he had never known. Reflecting on the impacts of the influential people in his life enabled Michael to see how their respective examples, both positive and negative, shaped him at all levels. From his Timeline, Michael discovered the commitments and convictions that emerged as important and non-negotiable. Over time, these ideas morphed into the values and beliefs currently directing his decisions, choices, and behaviors.

The defining moment of Awaken came when he was challenged to write a single statement that summed up his identity in the eyes of God. Essentially, he needed to answer the question: Who is Michael Vinings, based on the Word of God? Sifting through all the experience, the information, the knowledge, the influences, the preconceptions, the illusions, the truth, and the Savior, Michael finally concluded: "I am my Dad's boy. A son in his image."

Following Awaken, Michael experienced Activate, where he learned, for himself and ultimately for those he shepherds, how to live the sent life of a missionary in the natural rhythms of life.

Transformational. That was the only way in which Michael could describe the events of the three days. Being in God's presence for such an extended period of time, focusing in on the complex story that was his life, scrutinizing every detail, every opportunity, every blessing the Lord placed in his life...Michael knew he—and consequently his ministry—would never be the same. He was beyond excited to return home and share about this weekend—with anyone who would listen.

Before heading back on Thursday evening and preparing to dive head-long into the daily realities of life, Michael asked Stu and Gary if they would be available for a time of prayer. What transpired between the three of them was nothing short of a miraculous outpouring of God's Spirit. Tears flowed openly from Michael's eyes as Gary and Stu both laid hands on him and spoke prophetic words of blessing and authority over his ministry and church. Despite his emotional reaction, a profound awareness of peace settled into his spirit and planted an immovable confidence in him that carried over into the next weeks and months as Michael painstakingly implemented the precepts he had learned. The powerful wave of prayer eventually crested and subsided, until the three men sat in a congenial silence with one another, each man's hand grasping the should of the man next to him. It was then that Stu's deep voice broke the comfortable quiet. The soothing tones of his voice washed over the trio as he softly sang the chorus of an old, familiar hymn: "*How marvelous, how wonderful / And my song shall ever be / How marvelous, how wonderful / Is my Savior's love for me.*" All three men joined together in an off-key, yet utterly sincere version of the hymn, embraced once more, and said their good-byes.

***

Six weeks after attending the Awaken and Activate workshop, Michael received another mysterious package from Stu. This one was thin, Fed-Ex delivered, and undisturbed by Patricia. Throughout these past several weeks, Michael had experienced a comprehensive paradigm shift that was both incremental and intentional. He gently introduced one or two of his new ideas to his staff, simply for discussion. He still felt clueless, and slightly gun-shy, about moving toward implementation.

At this same time, Stu began gently shifting the focus of Michael's coaching from his personal development to the leadership of his congregation. Michael felt as if this package may have something to do with that shift, but he was unsure. He opened the envelope and extracted a business-looking letter from inside. It read:

Dear Michael,

As stewards of CRM's reFocusing process, we envision fresh and transformative movements of God in which individuals, families, and churches are fundamentally changed by discovering, embracing, and living out their unique and God-given calling to change the world in the name of Jesus. To see this type of transformation happen requires a marked shift in our thinking and understanding. We must shift . . .

. . . from Maintenance to Mission.

What if we, as a church, choose to define ourselves by something other than our Sunday morning gathering? What if our calling is not merely to take care of our own, but rather, to take care of the scores of not-yet-believers within our spheres of influence? What if we truly live empowered lives, which make a tangible difference in the world around us? To do so requires a move from merely maintaining the status quo to boldly pushing forward in the mission that Christ Himself started here on Earth. We believe the Church has both the calling and the capacity to press forward, empowered by God's Spirit, to see his Kingdom come, here on Earth.

100

... from Attraction to Engagement.

The reality is that in today's fast-paced, media-saturated culture, the Church is ill-equipped to compete for the attention and loyalty of the masses. Indeed, many in our society have become inoculated against and disenfranchised from the Good News of Christ, by the constant stream of marketing messages that inundate our lives. We believe that rather than jumping into the constant flow of attractive marketing, which screams, "Try this!" the Body of Christ has an opportunity to follow Jesus' example by authentically engaging and being with people. We have the opportunity to listen to them, rather than asking them to listen to us. We have the opportunity to go to them, rather than requiring them to come to us.

... from the Cultural Path to the Kingdom Path.

We must recognize that we are a spiritual people and a royal priesthood. As such, our values and decisions are not to be dictated by the culture in which we live. Rather, they are derived from our identity as citizens of the Kingdom of God. The cultural path is easy, indistinct, and it is popular. Life on the Kingdom Path is marked by deep dependence on God. It is often difficult, subtle, and lonely. Jesus stated, "narrow is the gate and difficult is the way which leads to life, and there are few who find it." (Matthew 7:14) As God's people, we *must* live out a different value system, a different ethic from the world around us. This is how they will know that we are his.

... from Lecture to Discovery.

If we truly believe Ephesians 2:10 ... that we are God's workmanship, and that He is preparing each of us for good works, then we must acknowledge the very real and active presence of God in the life of every believer. As such, we believe our role as apostolic leaders is not primarily to impart knowledge. Rather, our role is to help others discover the ways in which our Sovereign God has already been at work in them. This is a powerful and incredibly empowering mode of learning, as we are given freedom and the space needed to learn from the Spirit of God Himself. This type of learning truly produces life-change and transformation.

... from Doing to Being.

Perhaps the most revolutionary truth of the Gospel is that God's love for us, displayed in Christ, is total, complete, and all-encompassing ... and in no way tied to anything we could possibly do to earn it. While this is the truth of the Gospel, so many in the church struggle to live lives based on *being*, rather than *doing*. They stay busy, moving from one activity to another (in the name of Kingdom advancement), all the while failing to simply *be* with our Father. The end result is a life and ministry that are shadows of what they could be ... sustained only by their efforts and gifts, rather than by being truly powerful, spiritually authoritative, and ultimately world-changing. We must recognize that our identity and value comes from who we are, *not* what we do. We are God's beloved children, co-heirs with Christ, and the precious sheep of his pasture.

... from Caretaker to People Developer.

A vast majority of leaders in the local church lament the fact that an incredible amount of time is spent "putting out fires," rather than seeing significant ministry happen. In our language, we call that ministry "caretaking." In order to see real change leaders must get into the business of truly developing people. Leadership is *not* merely taking care of people in order to keep them happy and comfortable. Rather, leadership is confidently and intentionally stewarding both gifts and relationships to see people living empowered, bold lives that impact the world beyond. As leaders we must spend time encouraging, affirming, rebuking, and challenging those within our sphere of influence to live their calling to the glory of God the Father.

... from Gesturing to Committed Action.

Over the past several decades, the Church has surrendered its biblical injunction to be a transformative force in society. Rather than getting dirty and investing deeply over long periods of time in the uncomfortable places in our communities, many churches have become content to simply throw a little money at problems, or work to vote problem-makers out of office. Gestures are easy, infrequent activities that cost us very little. We may feel good about ourselves, but our activity produces little lasting change in the lives of the

103

recipients. This is not the life Jesus exemplified. The time for mere gestures is over. Now is the time for us as believers to take decisive, committed action to live out the reality of God's Kingdom in the midst of those outside our churches. The Lord desires to use us, his Bride, to answer the desperate prayers of the lost all around us. We must leap into action … with urgency, with resolve, and with the power and authority of God's Kingdom.

… from Independent Learner to Learning Community.

One of the greatest gifts the Lord has given is the gift of one another. We believe that there is great power in God's people learning with and from one another. Paul repeatedly refers to God's people as the Body of Christ. He describes the many ways we need one another in order to be successful. As we lead we want to fully leverage the gift of one another. We have seen God provide insights, answers, and new perspective through other people. Our learning and our growth must happen in the context of a safe, authentic learning community.

Michael, I would like to talk to you about the possibilities you are sensing as it pertains to leading your church forward as a mission. I've just outlined a series of deep and meaningful shifts for you to talk through with your fellow leaders and influencers. From our earliest conversations, it seems that most of your colleagues and a few select elders are already interested in discussing these shifts with you. I encourage you to engage in intentional discussion with them now. Being sensitive to the complexities of change, you and your leaders should explore these shifts together with mutual understanding and love for one another. Once you have had a chance to do this, contact me and we can begin to discuss a path forward, if you *and* your leaders want to implement these shifts.

Respectfully,

Stu

Michael sat quietly for a few moments, reflecting on the letter. Several worries floated through his mind. As excited as he had been about making a move, Michael now felt the claws of fear slowly working their way back into his heart. To accomplish these shifts would require more than a series of programs, classes, sermons, or nice ideas. This level of transformation would require a fundamental change all the way around the Body. It would necessitate a level of spiritual attention and awareness that his congregation currently did not possess.

Again, the magnitude of the situation ahead forced Michael to his knees. He devoted the following two days to prayer and fasting. After some intense listening during that time, he decided to make copies of Stu's letter for the weekly staff meeting and next week's elder's meeting. Additionally, he prepared a statement detailing all that had transpired since he initially connected with Stu (his journal came in handy here), as he sensed it would help him to express the deep work God accomplished in him, both as a minister and as a son. Both these documents would help him to clearly communicate to his brothers and sisters what he had learned … or at least he hoped they would.

Eight days later, a joint meeting with both staff and elders was scheduled. The night of the meeting was dark and deep. A few stars freckled the black sky. Michael came in early for the meeting so that he would have time to pray and prepare.

Michael leaned back in his office chair and looked at the ceiling. It was the same ceiling he had looked at in desperation almost a year ago. The ceiling that at one time seemed like a barrier now was a window through which vision seemed to pour from heaven.

Minutes passed and the clock ticked, and Michael waited. He glanced one more time out the window at the twinkling stars. They seemed to him to be some type of promise, just like the promise God gave to Abraham. Smiling, Michael rose from his desk and walked down the hall to the conference room, notes in hand for the meeting.

***

"Do we have any more chocolate milk?" shouted Carol over the shouts and laughter of about thirty-five kids eating lunch.

"I think so," answered Michael, and he ran to the break room of the library to check the refrigerator. Sure enough, a dozen cartons of chocolate milk sat on the second shelf. He grabbed three.

"Here, is this okay?" he asked. Carol nodded haphazardly—maybe to Michael or maybe to the four-year-old clinging to her leg begging for another apple. Nonetheless, she snatched the milk out of his hand and passed it over to a hungry girl sitting at the end of the table. Michael couldn't help but chuckle at Carol. With one tiny imp on her hip, another tugging at her shorts, and a thick strand of hair covering her eye and being continuously blown out of the way by her mouth, she looked the part of the ragged, over-worked mother. Except for the fact that she was beaming.

"Michael, we have ten more kids today. Ten more!" she exclaimed. "I never thought there would be such a need. I'm so glad we're doing this."

Indeed, Michael was also caught by surprise with the response to their Summer Lunch Program. When the staff and the elders agreed to move forward with some of Michael's (and Stu's) suggestions, one of the first proposals for connecting with the community came from Carol. In doing some research, Carol discovered that over the summer, thousands of low-income children went without eating lunch. These kids typically received free-and-reduced lunches at school, and now that they were home for the summer, their parents simply couldn't afford to feed them the extra meal. Carol learned about an opportunity to join forces with the local library (a place where these kids typically hang out) to provide lunches twice a week to whoever happened to show up.

Astonishingly, scores of people from the congregation jumped on board. Several donated the resources to purchase the food each week; the youth group got together on Sunday nights to pack the lunches; Jonathan tagged along once a week and brought his guitar to sing songs to (and with) the kids; Evan began contacting local businesses to get donations for food and other school supplies which the kids might need; and several small groups volunteered on a rotation to serve the lunches each week. In the meantime, a couple of individuals began making connections with the parents of these kids. It was just unbelievable.

Never in his wildest dreams did Michael think that his congregation would embrace something like this. In reality, there were several people who, in fact, did not embrace this or any of the changes Michael had proposed to the leadership. Sadly, those folks did not stick around long enough see the wholesome, plump, delicious fruit grow from the tree. And while those losses hurt deeply, Michael knew that even pruning was a part of producing good fruit.

As strains of a raucous version of "Jesus Loves the Little Children" drifted from the Children's Reading Room across the library, Michael's phone began to ring.

"Hello, this is Michael Vinings," he answered.

"Hello, Michael Vinings of Dallas, this is Stu Moyer," came the voice on the other end of the line.

"Hey Stu! How are you? What? I'm so sorry, I can't hear you right now. It's actually a little noisy…where am I? I'm at the library." Michael laughed out loud at the irony of his statement. "Yeah, yeah, it's going well, hold on a second…" He slipped into the bathroom and locked himself in a stall. "There, I think I'm safe now. What's up Stu?"

"Well, I was just calling to check in. It had been a while since our last conversation, and I wanted to know how things are going. From the sound of it, I'd say things are going pretty well."

Michael chuckled, "Yeah, I guess if I have to lock myself in a bathroom at the public library to get a little peace and quiet, it is going well. But seriously, Stu, we fed 47 kids today. We actually had to feed them in shifts because there wasn't enough room at the tables. Thank the Lord for Jonathan and his guitar. He totally entertains the ones who aren't eating."

"It's amazing what happens when you mobilize people to be the hands and feet of Jesus," observed Stu.

"Isn't it though?" responded Michael. "And Stu, I feel like this is just the start. I mean, I don't really have any other plans right now, and I know that's totally fine. But I also know that God is working on the heart of someone right now, and that in his time, something big…" he caught himself, "no, what I mean is something completely God-ordained will be revealed."

Feeling silly about hiding out in the bathroom, Michael emerged from his secret spot to a cacophony of squeals and giggles. The real miracle here was that the librarians allowed these kids to be so noisy! Once out of his hiding place, he was fair game. A swarm of kids encircled his knees, and one of them wrapped his arms around Michael's mid-section.

"Well, I don't want to keep you Michael. I'm sure you have your hands full. But I do want to touch base with you in no more than a week."

"Will do, Stu. Talk to you soon," and with that, he hung up and placed his phone in his shirt pocket. Then, with a fresh set of eyes and a fullness of joy in his heart, he looked endearingly at the Lilliputian crowd rapidly gathering around him. Taking in their giggles and smiles and openness, an idea popped into his head. "Who wants to hear a story?" he called out to the throng of wiggling bodies. "I've got the most wonderful story to tell you. It's about one of my best friends. His name is Jesus."

re|FOCUSING

Four Steps Toward Community Impact

How My Church Became Missional and Yours Can Too

FOUR STEPS TOWARD COMMUNITY IMPACT
Kirk Kirlin

Discover and follow these four steps to be a church that impacts your community.

For a couple of decades, my ministry team has been making pastors better leaders. The point isn't to run better programs or have slicker services, or to keep more and more people busy doing more and more religious activity.

It's to impact their cities the way Christ did.

I served at a successful church for several years. Just about every dime of our budget, minute of our time, and ounce of our collective energy was eaten up ministering on our campus to those who showed up. While we succeeded in gathering almost twelve hundred people, we missed almost 3,000,000 who lived and worked within reach. The money we spent on "outreach" we used to promote our events.

Two things make this upsetting. ONE: fewer and fewer Americans are willing to visit a church at any time, for any reason. TWO: Jesus and the early church didn't operate this way. Rather than promote weekly extravaganzas at Solomon's colonnade, Jesus met and ministered to people where they were.

Building relationships within the community and, ministering to those outside the congregation, creates a church that is thriving and vibrant.

We call churches like these, "missional churches." Isn't that what you would want your church to be?

There is a process that's doable, transferrable, and follows a few sequential steps. Want to know them? Read on.

"Being part of reFocusing has been life changing to me. Now, I focus on the joy of being a child of God whose value is not dependent on how many people show up to hear me preach. Before reFocusing my time was spent trying to do 900 things that weren't all that

1

important. Now, I concentrate on specific things God empowers me and calls me to do."

-D. Cook, Atlanta, GA

ONE: AWAKEN TO YOUR PERSONAL CALLING

Before your church can become missional, some of your members must live on- mission. Think of it this way: personal change precedes corporate change. When I say, "live on mission," I mean that these are people who sense God's calling to reach out into their communities and build relationships with unchurched people. And then they actually act on it. This "calling," we've found, is not nearly as mysterious as many assume.

God Uses Our Past

God knows what He's doing in our lives. Most of the time we're called to connect with non-Christians who are like us—those people who have similar backgrounds and experiences as our own. You might feel uniquely burdened for those who've experienced some of what you have. My friend Robert spent a very unpleasant childhood being shuffled from crummy foster home to abusive foster family until, as a teenager, he was adopted by a Christian couple. They loved and cared for him as no one had ever done. It

2

was transformational. He became an exceptional person, finishing UCLA Law and going on to own a thriving law practice.

But what's more, because of his own childhood and upbringing, he ended up founding and financing Christian orphanages in Nicaragua and the Philippines. His ministry, Arms of Love International, finds, embraces, loves, cares for, and holistically educates dozens of kids nobody wants. Do you see how God shaped him to make an incredible and unique impact?

Ephesians 2:10 says: "For we are God's handiwork, created in Christ Jesus to do good works, which God prepared in advance for us to do."

If this is true, then all your life experiences have been orchestrated to shape you for the "good" that you get to do. Discovering your missional calling is often as easy as looking carefully over your life: the people, the events, and the circumstances that have made you, "you".

Wondering if you're where you're supposed to be? Consider your skills, connections, experiences, passions, and concerns. Let them direct you toward where you're to serve. Think about how God might use you, like Robert, in a unique way.

"*God has awakened in me the understanding that I am a work in progress which need not be finished in order to be used – unpolished features and all – right now for God's purposes. I am usable at this very moment. God loves me and will not let me fail – he causes my talents, values, desires for His glory. He has re-awakened in me the desire to serve Him and others at a doable level. I have gotten so much out of the reading, writing, and discussion. Now, I need to give back, working with what I have learned. I want to have an impact on my community and now I know it is possible, despite the barriers I may put up, or cling to. Thank you.*"
-L. Howat, All Saints Anglican Church

"*Simply put, the reFocusing process has been a profound gift to me personally. As the new pastor with a lot to prove, my work with you has given me the ability to take the attention off myself and place it where it belongs - on the development of strong leaders who can invite our congregation into greater faithfulness and effective mission.*"
-Rev. M. Murray

TWO: ACTIVATE YOUR PERSONAL CALLING

Even when armed with a clear and concise sense of missional calling, relatively few Christians make the jump from sitting in church to living like a missionary in their local context.

4

Most need a pretty powerful "nudge" to break loose from the momentum of the life they're accustomed to and the commitments that consume their time. This step can be hard—many well-intentioned church members are so busy with church activities that they don't have time to minister to those outside.

So, how do we step into our new, missional calling?

1.   Assess Your Commitments

List your current commitments, and think about each one. Is the commitment in line with the missional calling you feel God has for you? Does this commitment take too much of your time without furthering your impact on those you care about? Some commitments may need modification, while others may need to be removed altogether.

2.   Recognize Your Spheres

For Ephesians 2:10 to be true, that God has been shaping us all along for what He's planned for us to do, God will have provided both the people to help us move into our missional calling and the people we're meant to serve and influence. Who are some of the people that might help you move into your calling? Who are some of the people you feel called to serve? It's beneficial to consider those in your relationship sphere who are God's provision for you in both roles.

3.   Take Action

This is the step that seems so much easier said than done. But here's the thing: without a concerted, deliberate leap, we can never hurdle all that binds us to the comforts of the life we know. We have to break out of the familiar to begin connecting with those to whom we're called. We have to actually act. The commitments that you've decided are superfluous time-fillers that actually diminish the missional living God's called you to? Get rid of them. Make the calls you need to make. Delegate responsibility. And once you've made the decision to take that leap, you can keep connecting, serving, blessing, and loving the people you're called to.

To illustrate the leap, consider the example of Dave, a denominational executive burdened with the oversight of 65 churches in his district. Before taking Step Two, he routinely worked 70-hour weeks and had no connection to anyone unchurched. During the Activate Workshop, Dave found ways to gradually cut more than 20 hours from his workweek. This freed Dave up to meet his neighbors, and over the course of shared coffee and meals, Dave and those neighbors created a deep friendship. Now, a couple years later, they regularly call on Dave in times of stress or distress and are moving toward Christ in unprecedented ways.

How Does This Impact My Church?

6

Remember what we talked about in Step One? Personal change precedes corporate change. You can only help your church understand its calling if you've walked through the steps yourself. Once you've begun acting on your own missional calling. Impacting those outside the church, you can lead your church to become missional. But how does that work? Keep reading…

"The reFocusing process was transformational for me as a leader and for our church. I am in my first senior pastorate leading a church that is over 60 years old. Over time, the church slipped into a maintenance mode and I possessed neither the knowledge nor courage to lead the church into effective outward-focused community impacting ministry.

The Assess and Advance Workshops helped us develop a practical disciple-making process to support people's growth into maturity in Christ. This process was nothing short of transformational for me as a leader and for our congregation. I am a much stronger, more com- petent leader than I was before reFocusing. I am more hopeful about our church's future than I ever have been. This process was a game-changer for me and will continue to bear fruit for the rest of my life and ministry."

-Pastor D. Adwalpalker, California

THREE: ASSESS YOUR CHURCH'S CALLING

Just as Ephesians 2:10 applies to individuals, we've found it is applicable to churches: *"For we are his workmanship..."* While it's great that individual believers are connecting with the unchurched in meaningful ways, a congregation serving together on local mission can change a city. A few years ago, a city councilwoman confessed regarding influence of a local church in her city: "I don't know where our city would be without this church. They've contributed to our city in ways we could never repay!"

But where is your church equipped to serve? Here are several small steps to discern where God is calling your church to impact the community.

1.   Analyze Your "Mission Field"

To determine who God has prepared your congregation to serve in the local community and the unique, redemptive impact you're best equipped to make, some analysis of your "mission field" is valuable. Have a few church members interview community leaders (chief of police, school principals, city council members, community service administrators, and the mayor's office). The objective is to learn the local residents' hopes, dreams, worries, and concerns. They should also ask about barriers to Christ, the gospel, and the Church in that community. Others can obtain demographic data on both the community and the congregation.

8

2.   Discover the Relationship between the Church and the Community

It's really helpful to gather the congregation to consider the character and nature of the relationship the church has had with the community throughout its history. When has it been cooperative? Combative? Deeply engaged? Distant and isolated? What are the most prominent events, people, and circumstances that articulate the dynamic nature of this relationship? This process is often rich with insights about how and how not to engage the community.

3.   Understand Your Makeup

Consider the overlap and the outliers between the demographic makeup of the congregation and the community. In determining your "mission focus," the key question is: where and how can we serve people like us who are not yet Christian? We know this runs counter to the conventional wisdom, which is to focus your energies on the "least of these." But here's the thing. When you seek to build relationships with people who are unlike you, they are often uncomfortable, guarded, and distrusting—even more than normal.

If your church is a well-educated, upper-middle class, suburban congregation, those you'd like to impact in the inner city will not be drawn to you. But, residents, who are like you, in your community will. This is not to suggest that God cannot call a church to serve outside its own demographic, but rather to encourage you to look first toward your own community.

Laguna Niguel, CA is one of those suburbs that gives the appearance that residents haven't a care in the world—nice cars and immaculate lawns line its streets. Treating homelessness or poverty wasn't an option for the local churches. Instead, as a part of Step Three, a Presbyterian church interviewed the City Council to determine where it could serve. Partnering with the Red Cross, members became disaster preparedness advocates in their neighborhoods. Helping neighbors to be ready for wildfires, floods, and earthquakes—disasters common to this area—they forged lasting relationships and met practical needs.

A Christian Church in the L.A. basin is a mix of Anglo, Hispanic, and Filipino, some of whom are on the edge of poverty. Most are underemployed, and some are unemployed. They learned of a community of people who'd lost their homes and were living in their cars, RV's and campers.

They adopted this community and, almost weekly, found tangible ways to serve, befriend, and love these resilient people. Westside was able to connect deeply with people who had lost everything. Today, many of them have a relationship with Christ and deep friendships with the members of the church.

Discerning God's calling for your church, looking at the needs of the community and deciding how your church can serve those needs is vital to becoming the vibrant church God wants all churches to be, something we'll discuss more in Step Four.

> *"When it comes to releasing the missional DNA in congregations, reFocusing has the tools to Awaken and Activate followers of Jesus to live a life of mission."*
> -Alan Hirsch, Missiologist and Author

FOUR: ADVANCE YOUR CHURCH'S CALLING

Every pastor or church leader wants the church to be vibrant, growing, and healthy. Unfortunately, that desire can lead us to over-focus on ourselves, instead of the ministry the church does in the community. Once the process of determining some possible areas your church could affect the community is completed), it's now time to actually make that happen.

1.   Focus

Nothing is more essential to a church's missional strategy than to impact community residents regularly, repeatedly, redemptively, and unconditionally. But, it's not the amount of activity that matters; it's the impact you're having.

"Every pastor or church leader wants the church to be vibrant, growing, and healthy. Unfortunately, that desire can sometimes focus work on the church itself, instead of the ministry the church does in the community."

When a congregation begins to living on mission, there's a strong temptation to go in all directions at once. Once your eyes are opened, you discover there are so many needs and so many ways to help! It's critical to resist the impulse to dibble and dabble all over town. Instead, pick one place, one people to engage frequently, generously, and beneficially.

For example, about a third of the congregation of a Free Methodist Church in California's South Bay are seniors, so they decided to adopt a residential care facility for retirees. Every week, church members care for residents, family members, and staff at the Care Center. While their involvement includes a weekly bible study, their engagement is not overtly religious in nature. They throw birthday parties, holiday events, and staff appreciation barbeques. On a regular basis, they meet the needs of residents and staff practically, emotionally, relationally, and spiritually. Recently, an administrator commented that in his twenty-year career he's never seen a church care so deeply, regularly, and beneficially. He recently said, if this continues, "I might change my religion."

2.   Serve for Their Benefit, Not Ours

Step Four centers on deciding where to go and what to do in order to regularly serve unchurched folks for their benefit. This is not "outreach" as commonly conceived. It isn't intended to get people to join your church.

In fact, it's not intended to get people to do anything. What it does is provide a context for believers to present the Gospel to demonstrate who, otherwise, would not experience it.

A suburban Foursquare decided to adopt their church city offices, offering free volunteers for any civic function. At first their offers fell flat. City officials were skeptical that church members would manipulate this opportunity to promote itself and button-hook guests into one-sided religious debates. After months of saying "no," the city had a need for volunteers they could not fill any other way.

When church members came and served without wearing church logo shirts, without hanging a banner advertising their service times and location, and without handing out 'Come Worship With Us' cards—the City was relieved. The church was invited back…again and again. Careful to love and serve the city for its benefit alone, the church developed a reputation for being authentic, caring, and generous. Relationships formed. Trust developed. In time, several city employees gave their lives to Christ, and some are now regulars at the church.

3.   Work as a Team

To become a vibrant church that reaches the community, you'll need to establish a committed leadership team and a team leader for each missional initiative. These people do the initial work of building relationships with the administrators, supervisors, and executives where your congregation will be serving. They'll provide the leadership, communicate ministry opportunities and successes, and invent ways for the congregation to participate broadly and deeply in the missional initiative.

In our years working with churches, we've found the importance of two priorities. One, the governing body of the church (elder board, trustees, etc.) needs to commit itself to the fulfillment of the mission plan that results from Steps Three and Four. Commonly, this requires a negotiated hand-off between the lay leadership team that's been championing the process through the first four steps and the governing board. This happens best when it's the only agenda item for a full day meeting of the church staff, lay leadership team, and governing board. Once the handoff is complete, the lay team can be disbanded.

Two, a high-visibility, high-priority all-church launch event is the best way to kick off the first missional initiative and garner widespread support by the congregation. Schedule it a few months after your leadership team has begun to serve people at that site: public school, sheriff's department, Boys & Girl's club, etc. This way, you'll have already made a positive impact there—an impact the recipients of your service will be enthusiastic to talk about. Invite the school principal, sheriff, or administrator to address your congregation and say whatever they want about what you've just begun to do. Even skeptics in the congregation will have difficulty refuting the beneficial fruit that's already begun to blossom. If you have multiple weekend services, consider combining them—maybe in the parking lot of the place you've begun to serve. Conclude with a potluck or barbeque for your people and those to whom you've begun to minister.

Why Is This Important?

We live at a moment in Church history when deep change is underway, both in the culture and in the Church. The "attractional model" that served us well for much of the last 50 years is much less effective today. Some would argue it doesn't work at all. Not here. Not anywhere. More than any time in US history, people are not looking for a church. Much of society has decided that we don't have what they need, so they stay away. In droves.

They need to experience the Gospel. To see it lived out in ways that impact their lives, overcome their skepticism, and thaw their cynicism. Only love—generous and unconditional love—will do that.

One last example: A mid-sized Methodist Church has taken all four steps. Realizing they had a number in their congregation who work in law enforcement and discovering their community is home to three prisons, they adopted the correctional officers at a State prison just a half-mile from the church. A team was formed and began to lead the congregation as it invented ways to express appreciation and admiration for the prison guards. Over many months, the church has been caring, helping, and serving those officers—even while external pressures produced gross overcrowding, a riot by inmates, job cuts, and an extended lock down of the facility.

Not long ago, an official confessed that because of this congregation's influence, "the environment has changed" in the prison. Correctional officers, impacted by the kindness and care of church members are different. They now relate to the inmates in new ways. And this has changed the way the inmates are with each other.

Could it be that the Kingdom of God has come to this prison? Is the Kingdom of God ready to break into your community?

What is your church's impact? What could it be?

NEED HELP WITH THE STEPS OR WANT TO DISCUSS YOUR POSSIBILITIES?

To learn more, please visit our website at www.reFocusing.org or contact us at reFocusing@crmleaders.org.

HOW MY CHURCH BECAME MISSIONAL,
AND HOW YOURS CAN TOO

A Story From Darren, A Pastor In California.

I was unprepared for the mountain of expectations I faced stepping into a 60-Year Old Church.

It stood in stark contrast to my previous role as a church planter. There, I set the expectations that my role as pastor would primarily be that of equipper of the saints for ministry to those outside the church.

But I was wrong. Taking this church was like stepping onto a treadmill of internally focused projects (budgets, facilities, ailing members and poorly functioning programs) that I was expected to perpetuate.

The amount of work that it took to keep this programming going left very little time and energy to build meaningful relationships with anyone outside the church.

Initially, there was a lot of talk about 'reaching out' to our community. But, I quickly learned that this meant 'getting them to come here' to be part of our programs.

I'd run between meetings, hospital beds, and home visits always with church members. As long as I did, there was general approval of my ministry provided that I was always busy and church finances were strong.

During reFocusing's Missional Pathway Training, I started wondering if this is really what ministry was to be all about. Is our 'outreach' to be focused on getting the unchurched to join us in what we're doing?

Are we making a true impact in our community?'

I started to imagine how my role as a pastor could shift from caretaking church members to equipping them to make an impact outside the church through practical service and genuine relationship.

Naively, I assumed long-time followers of Jesus would be excited to serve those outside. I didn't anticipate that so many would passively resist these changes or leave the church entirely.

Honestly, I was shocked and dismayed by the strength of opposition, especially from those who'd been leaders in the congregation.

Rebounding from the stinging criticisms that came when we terminated cherished programs that merely served ourselves, I gathered a team of enthusiastic people who'd previously been on the margins of the church. This team led our effort to serve the staff and residents at a local convalescent facility.

Through our ministry of presence, prayer and encouragement, we've seen the Gospel of the Kingdom take hold in the lives of many at the senior center.

And, some of the greatest impact has been on team members who regularly visit the convalescent home. Their joy, renewed faith, and enthusiasm for Christ has been palpable and contagious. I've never seen a church program or Sunday school class produce this kind of growth in people's lives. It's been encouraging to see spiritual growth replicated in other lives as we continue to find ways to engage our community with the Gospel.

5 TIPS TO PASTORS FROM DARREN:

1.   BECOME A CHANGE AGENT

As pastor, the most important part of becoming a change agent has been learning to manage my own reactivity. The clearer I've become in presenting the vision to the congregation, the clearer people became about whether they wanted to be a part of it or not. Some left. Others stopped giving.

Criticism abounded, and this was particularly unsettling because I'd always been a people-pleaser. I was tempted to dampen the focus on community-based impact by softening my approach from the pulpit and in conversations with people.

However, as I continued to function an agent of change, I became convinced that in order to experience the deep level of influence that God intends us to have in this community, I must die to my need for others' approval.

Leading in this context required me to release the unrealistic expectation that I could somehow lead change so well that everyone would like me.

2.   WORK WITH RESISTANCE AND DON'T TAKE IT PERSONALLY

I learned that some people have trained themselves to resist change, and they were responding exactly as they'd been trained. This perspective helped me interpret the intransigence more as a reflection on their posture toward change than a referendum on my leadership.

3.   CRITICISM BRINGS CLARITY

I have learned to accept criticism as a gift that brings clarity. Criticism reveals what I'm willing to suffer for. After many lengthy, fruitless conversations with leaders and members who were intent on returning to a paradigm of congregant-focused ministry, I became convinced that there's no going back.

4.   RETREAT IS NOT AN OPTION

The road ahead may be uncertain, but one thing is clear: retreat is not an option. Through the change process, my character has been tested and refined. My capacity to 'stand' in the midst of anxiety has deepened. My vision has been sharpened, as has the courage to communicate it plainly.

5.   CONTINUE TO SERVE OUTWARD

I've also learned to remain vigilant in fighting the magnetic pull toward inward-serving organizational maintenance if I'm to lead this body of believers to make a lasting impact for Christ. While I haven't always enjoyed the painful process of leading my congregation (and myself) through change, I wouldn't trade the gains we've made in personal transformation and congregational maturity for a less difficult path.

Kirk Kirlin, one of the reFocusing team specialist, writes his story about Darren.

The move to become a missional church was challenging for Darren, Senior Pastor at a church in Southern California. After committing themselves to the reFocusing's MISSIONAL PATHWAY training event many in the church resisted efforts to shift the church's focus from caring for itself to caring for those outside the church in the local community.

The tension grew as the preference for mission displaced the emphasis on merely entertaining and educating existing church members. Eventually, key leaders in the ministry resigned their leadership roles and some left the church entirely. At the same time, a number of regular members of the congregation were "catching fire". After experiencing the AWAKEN AND ACTIVATE WORKSHOPS, several began to intentionally build relationships with unchurched people in their community. Near the end of the reFocusing process, the church adopted a struggling senior care facility (LCC) nearby, serving lower income retirees.

Recently, an administrator wrote that, "in a career spanning more than 20 years, he's never seen a church serve those outside so consistently, generously, and selflessly. If it continues", he added, "he might change his religion."

As stories of the growing responsiveness of LCC staff and residents filtered through the church, much of the criticism from long-standing church members and elders has been silenced. More members are beginning to engage the missional initiatives, and God is bringing new people to the church who are gleefully engaging in the pastor's disciple-development efforts and its ministry in the city.

In addition, the church has launched a second initiative, championed by the Spanish-speaking congregation, ministering to itinerant day laborers in the parking lots of three local hardware stores .

Church members provide friendship, food, and prayer on a regular basis. At the time of this writing, a third missional initiative is underway to partner with 13 other churches in the community to serve as a shelter for homeless families.

These outward focused ministries evidence that the missional culture is becoming the prevalent DNA of this congregation. The church has experienced a spiritual renewal. Serving the community with no strings attached becomes the 'new normal'. A deeper passion for worship and discipleship has developed as a necessary means of

providing 'fuel' for reaching out to others. Becoming a
church on mission has given this previously plateaued
congregation new life and vitality.

It will do the same for yours. Are you ready to begin the journey?

CRM works to create movements of committed followers

of Jesus by pioneering new ground among the unreached

and unchurched, bringing lasting transformation among

the poor, and mobilizing the Church for mission.

New Ground
Pioneering new ground among
the unreached and unchurched

The Poor
Bringing transformation
among the poor

The Church
Mobilizing the Church
for mission

CRM Empowering Leaders
1240 N. Lakeview Av #120
Anaheim, CA 92807
www.crmleaders.org

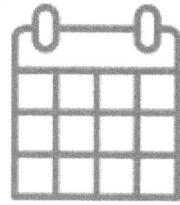

We Want To Help You Become Missional

Help your church get outside the walls of the church to impact your community. Let us walk with you every step of the Missional Pathway.

Feeling Isolated? Stay Connected.

A blog written by pastors and leadership specialists to help you stay current, encouraged, and resourced.

reFocusing Events

Our team is passionate about connecting with you personally. Come to the next training near your city and get trained in a process that is helping hundreds of other churches become missional.

re|FOCUSING

refocusing.org

facebook.com/crmrefocusing

@crmrefocusing

www.ingramcontent.com/pod-product-compliance
Lightning Source LLC
Chambersburg PA
CBHW060936040426
42445CB00011B/888